VETERINARY ADVICE FOR

Dog owners

A COMPLETE HOME REFERENCE GUIDE

Dick Lane BSc, FRAgS, FRCVS

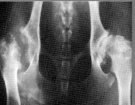

DEDICATION
For Maple, Maddy and Max.

ACKNOWLEDGEMENTS
The publishers would like to acknowledge the following for help with photography: Dick Lane and Angela Tyrrel.
The author would like to thank the following for help with the text: Angela Maclean, Anja Schmidt, June McNicholas
and many other veterinary surgeons.

Special thanks to Hills for use of line drawings from *Hills Atlas of Veterinary Clinical Anatomy* (© Hills).
Cover Photography: Top Sequence, left to right: © www.comstock.com; © www.comstock.com;
© istockphoto.com/Steve Dangers; © www.comstock.com.
Bottom sequence, left to right: © www.comstock.com; © Westline Publishing;
© www.comstock.com; © www.comstock.com.

A NOTE ON GENDER
The 'he' pronoun is used throughout this book instead of
the rather impersonal 'it', but no gender bias is intended.

DISCLAIMER
While every endeavour has been made to ensure that the content of this book is factually correct,
new research and developments in veterinary science mean that treatments and medication are
continually changing. Readers are advised always to consult their veterinary surgeon for advice. This
book is not a substitute for proper advice from a qualified professional, and neither the publisher
nor the author can assume any liability for any injury or damage.

First published in 2010 by The Pet Book Publishing Company Limited
PO Box 8, Lydney, Gloucestershire GL15 6YD

© 2010 Pet Book Publishing Company Limited.

All rights reserved
No part of this book may be reproduced or transmitted in any form or by any means, electronic or
mechanical, including photocopying, recording, or by any information storage and retrieval system,
without permission in writing from the publisher.

ISBN
978-1-906305-26-0
1-906305-26-9

Printed and bound in Singapore.

CONTENTS

FOREWORD

Several years ago, at the awards ceremony of the British Small Animal Veterinary Congress, a brand new award was presented – the *J.A. Wight Memorial Award*.

This honour, presented by the Blue Cross animal welfare charity in memory of my father, Alfred Wight (better known as James Herriot), is now presented annually to recognise outstanding contributions to the welfare of pet animals. I have the privilege of presenting this award each year, and the very first recipient on that day in Birmingham 2000 was Dick Lane.

As a most respected member of his profession, having spent a large proportion of his professional life supporting, among many others, charities such as Guide Dogs for the Blind and Dogs for the Disabled, it was entirely appropriate that Dick should be the first to receive the award. For me, it was especially satisfying that Dick Lane was to be the man to whom I was to present the award for the very first time.

Back in 1997, with little previous experience as a writer, and having taken on the task of writing the authorised biography of James Herriot, my initial surge of enthusiasm for the project was being replaced by serious misgivings about having sacrificed my work as a veterinarian to tackle the daunting prospect of writing a book. It was at this time, completely unexpectedly, I received words of encouragement from Dick. He had read about my undertaking in the *Daily Mail*, and expressed his "admiration for my courage on attempting the biography".

At that time I did not know Dick at all, but those words from a fellow veterinarian did much to set me back on track. As I presented Dick with his award at the BSAVA Congress, it seemed very fitting that it was the first occasion that we were to meet.

James Herriot endeared himself to his public through his compassionate and caring approach to his patients, and to his customers. He, of course, was just one of thousands of vets totally dedicated to the welfare of animals – and Dick Lane is another. Dick is a man who, despite having been the senior partner for 41 years in a busy veterinary practice in Leamington Spa, managed to find the time to help a host of organisations supporting animals and people less fortunate than himself. It is this wide experience with so many aspects of his profession that comes through in the pages of this book.

Veterinary medicine has made enormous progress since the days that Dick first qualified back in 1953. There are now so many ancillary aids available to the vet X-rays, ultrasound, blood biochemistry – that the vet can almost diagnose a condition without even touching the animal. Dick Lane worked through an era when the only available aids were the veterinary surgeon's eyes, his hands and his brain. This engenders a thorough,

Dick Lane has devoted much of his working life to Guide Dogs for the Blind and Dogs for the Disabled.

basic clinical approach, and Dick's book has resulted from years of *practical* experience, and is written in a straightforward, easy-to-understand text.

Modern veterinary practice is a stressful occupation. Long consulting hours can be exhausting, and this can be made worse for the veterinary surgeon when he has to explain every detail to a client with little or no knowledge of disease conditions that can afflict their pet. Life is so much easier for the vet when he is dealing with a well-informed owner, and this is just one example of the benefits resulting from the reading of this book.

Dick Lane and James Herriot have much in common. Both have been men who made time for others, and both have displayed total dedication to the good of their patients. Each of them worked through multiple years of veterinary practice, gaining invaluable experience. This is borne out, not only in the books of James Herriot, but also in Dick Lane's most practical and informative book. Anyone who has, as a priority, the well-being of all creatures great and small should find space on their shelves for this book. I wish it well.

Jim Wight BVMS MRCVS
Thirsk, North Yorkshire

PART I

PREVENTATIVE HEALTH CARE

THE HEALTHY DOG

Chapter 1

Most dogs are obtained as puppies purchased from a breeder at about eight weeks of age. The puppy is delightful, mischievous and may not be clean in the house. You must be prepared for a puppy to alter your lifestyle as well as making allowances for his ways. The puppy will occupy most of your day; he will be a friend, a source of amusement – and he will be dependent on you for all his needs, which will include his food and upbringing.

Problems are likely to develop when the new owner does not give sufficient time and attention to produce a well-behaved, desirable dog. There are also risks of illness if the feeding is incorrect or if preventive measures are overlooked. Vaccinations against common infectious diseases, worming at intervals, and treatment to combat skin parasites will all have to be considered – and the eventual cost may be more than the initial purchase price.

RESCUED DOGS

Some dogs are acquired as older puppies or adults. With a crossbred puppy – who has parents of different breeds – it could be a lucky dip as to how he will grow, but he may turn out to be healthier than a purebred pedigree. A mongrel puppy – where the breeding of the parents is unknown – will certainly be a surprise package in terms of size and temperament, but there are many fit and healthy mongrels that make excellent pets.

If you adopt from a rescue shelter, you will give a dog a chance to get out of kennels and become a family companion. The advantages of adopting a rescued dog are that adult size and temperament can be judged more easily and house training will usually be sorted out. However, there is a greater risk of unsatisfactory behaviour traits being established and patience will be needed to provide a good home background to help overcome such faults.

In the situation where the older dog comes through a friend or a relative (often elderly), some idea of the routine of feeding and exercise will be available. A dog coming through rescue kennels will be used to a kennel existence, but once in a home again will assume the routine he was used to in his former home. However, the 'lifestyle' between two homes may be considerably different. Praise for good actions and positive reinforcements must be given in the first weeks to help the dog settle in to his new home.

If you take on a rescued dog, you will need to help him settle into a new routine.

SIGNS OF HEALTH

You need to be familiar with a dog in good health to be able to recognise when a dog is becoming ill or is deteriorating with old age or disease. The experienced dog owner will remember how previous dogs acted or performed and will know almost instinctively that their dog is unwell. For the first-time owner there is no comparison possible and advice from others can be unhelpful at times. Meeting other dog owners on walks or out in the park will always allow friendships to strike up, but some remarks about diet and training may be contrary to present-day best practice for dogs. A few basic facts on dog health will not be wasted.

APPETITE

The way the dog eats is one of the easiest measures of health. Just after being weaned from their mother's milk, puppies are often over fed. Healthy pups are willing to consume all of the appetising food placed in front of them, and, with the competition of other littermates, the pup who can eat the quickest gets the most. Obviously this allows him to grow quicker and, being strongest, he is able to push his way into the food bowl, displacing the weaker siblings to the sidelines. The appetite is satisfied and the puppy has learnt to fight to succeed. He has learnt that food and eating is the quickest route to dominating others. The situation changes as soon as the puppy leaves the breeder and becomes a single puppy in a new home where there is no longer competition from littermates.

An older dog too will be used to a routine of food placed in front of him at a set time and will eat in a more calculated manner. Some dogs can become very choosy with their food and will walk away after a few mouthfuls, knowing there will be more food there whenever the dog chooses to come back. It is best not to pander to the reluctant feeder, but any sudden loss of appetite can show there is a health problem. Tooth decay, causing mouth pain, would seem one such reason. But an early lesson for owners of older dogs is that advanced dental disease and loose teeth seldom stop a dog eating; there are different levels of mouth pain in humans to dogs.

WEIGHED IN

One of the best ways of measuring a dog's food intake and his appetite is to weigh it using suitable scales, not always easy to find with larger breeds! Calculating the weight allows you to see if the poor or shy feeder is taking in enough food to maintain his bodyweight. Even more importantly, the first signs of becoming overweight can be noticed and excessive food intake reduced early enough for the dog not to suffer. There are now more problems in dogs of heart and joint diseases caused by obesity than from illness from semi-starvation in modern society.

When considering appetite as a way of confirming a dog's health, there is no reliable diet standard (such as half a kilogram of prepared food a day for a 'medium size' dog). Intake of food depends on the following factors:
• Age
• Activity levels
• Breed
• Temperament.

Traditionally, an adult dog was fed only one meal a day; there is now the possibility of putting down pelleted food for dogs to feed on through the day as they wish. The best control is using the weighing scales to stop overeating. Bodyweight is easily measured and is often a reliable guide to overall condition.

HEALTH MEASUREMENTS
As well as keeping a check on weight, there are a number of other health items that can be measured. They include body temperature, the breathing rate, and the speed of the heart (since the pulse is too rapid to count without instruments).

TEMPERATURE
A dog's temperature can be taken if a fever is suspected or if there is a sudden tiredness and lack of response and lethargy. The normal temperature of the adult is 38.3 to 38.7 Celsius (an

When a puppy arrives in his new home, he will have to adapt to feeding without the competition of his littermates.

average in Fahrenheit of 101.3). The newborn puppy may be as low as 94 to 97 F (35 to 37 C) at birth, but warms up depending on his environment.

A single raised temperature measurement may not be alarming. As with human measurements, try to follow the pattern by repeating the temperature taking after two to three hours. A continuing rise of temperature can be serious and a persistently low temperature would also be a cause for concern.

NORMAL HEART RATE
• Adult dogs: 60 to 120 beats a minute

• Toy breeds: up to 200 beats a minute
• Newborn puppy: 160 to 200 at birth increasing to 220 beats a minute at two weeks old.

The heart rate will always increase during and after vigorous exercise but should return to a normal level within five minutes.

NORMAL RESPIRATORY RATE
In an adult dog, just over 20 breaths a minute at rest, but the rate can vary between 10 and 30 breaths a minute. Panting from a need to lose heat or to bring oxygen to the lungs can be very rapid indeed. If in doubt, look at the colour of the tongue and the

TAKING YOUR DOG'S TEMPERATURE

A hand applied to the dog's head or body may give an impression of coolness or fever; the only effective way to measure your dog's temperature is to use a rectal thermometer. This may be a digital thermometer or the old-fashioned glass and mercury one that was more likely to break, especially if the dog or puppy is wriggly. Mercury is a poisonous substance and the EU has banned its use. Digital thermometers are safer and easier to read.

If still using the glass bulb thermometer, practise shaking it down until the mercury level registers 96 F (36 C). Turn your back to the light and rotate the glass slightly so the mercury column acts like a thin mirror reflecting the light and length towards you so you know the reading. Having practised reading the mercury column a few times, prepare to take the dog's temperature. Unless you know your dog well and he is very still, it is safest to have someone to steady the dog's front while you approach the dog's tail.

- First lubricate the bulb with Vaseline (petroleum) jelly or use KY jelly.
- Then lift the dog's tail and hold it to stop the dog suddenly sitting down.
- Insert the bulb into the anus with a slight rotary movement. This need be no deeper than the length of the digital or mercury bulb or as much as an inch, depending on the size of the dog.
- A 'half minute' mercury thermometer should be held in the rectum for almost a minute, less long for the digital variety.
- Remove the thermometer, wipe it clean and read the number by the silver length in the glass as previously practised.
- With a digital thermometer follow the maker's instructions, but all types are best cleaned after use with an alcohol or disinfectant wipe. Don't put a soiled thermometer away in its case.

Note: For newborn puppies there are special paediatric thermometers to use, and lower reading thermometers may also be useful in the older, inactive dog.

moistness of the mouth for reassurance (see below).

THE MOUTH

The tongue may not be the easiest place to assess when looking at the colour of the mucous membranes. The best plan is to raise the upper lips gently and examine the gums just above the upper canine tooth. A moist, pale pink colour is normal. Pale gums may be a sign of anaemia, or a narrowing of the capillary blood vessels due to pain, fear, shock, or loss of some body fluids. An ashen grey colour is a dangerous sign; a brick red colour indicates some toxaemia or poisoning (see page 52). Some dogs naturally have dark pigment on their gums.

URINE AND FAECAL OUTPUT

There are no real rules to follow, as the type of diet and thirst will affect consistency and output. Passing faeces once a day is considered normal in healthy adults; puppies produce more frequently. Voiding faeces often follows the eating of a meal. Within 30 minutes of a dog consuming a dried, pelleted type of food, the bowels may be ready to empty if the opportunity is provided. Dogs that have frequent 'snacks' or are fed 'on demand' may have different

A healthy mouth, showing clean teeth and pink gums.

Bright eyes are a good indicator of health and wellbeing.

needs with regards to eliminating waste. The fibre content of the food also affects the frequency of defecation – increased moist fibre in the diet promotes more frequent bowel movement.

Some bitches can hold urine in their bladders for 12 hours or more; male dogs, in contrast, feel obliged to mark every vertical object they pass with a few drops of urine. This urination pattern relates to social behaviour, and bitches coming near to breeding may suddenly start passing urine more frequently.

A common behavioural trait is submissive urination, which is more likely to occur in youngsters. The dog or bitch passes small amounts of urine when upset or stressed. In the presence of a dominant dog or person, the dog may roll on to his back and express a little pool of urine as a visible sign of submission.

Incontinence is loss of voluntary control over the act of passing urine and, infrequently, of faeces. Incontinent dogs wet the bed or make mistakes in the house. Such 'events' may indicate a health problem (see p. 67).

EYES
In good health, the eyes are one of the best places to watch. The dog should be alert, the eyes clear with no cloudiness, and only a little of the third eyelid visible in the corners. The conjunctiva (or 'white' of the eye) should be pink but never red. The eyes should appear slightly moist, but there should be no sticky mucus on the eye and no overflow of tears (often appearing as a brown tear streak on the face). The eyelids should lie smoothly on the eyeball surface with the eyelashes pointing outwards.

EARS
Ears will be held upwards for some breeds, but will droop down on the side of the face in other breeds. The head will move towards the source of any sound. There should be no smell from the ear canal, only a very small quantity of brown wax, and no discharge or matted fur obstructing the ear canal.

PART I

Pricked ears.

Drop ears that lie close to the head.

Rose ears.

The nose should be free from crustiness or discharge.

NOSE
The nose may be pigmented, but the two nostrils should be visible and not blocked by any crust or discharge. A slight moistness or clear runniness licked away is not unusual in cold weather.

SKIN AND COAT
The skin and coat varies with each breed. Bare or bald areas should not occur. Matted fur and raw areas indicate that a skin disorder may be present. The coat should smell fresh and is usually odour free.

FEET
The feet should carry the weight of each quarter of the body evenly; leg length varies from breed to breed. The toes are usually visible and the nails should not look overgrown. There should be no staining of the fur between the toes, as this is often due to saliva from licking.

MOVEMENT
When moving, the legs should work in harmony and any tendency to limp or favour a leg can be a cause for concern. Early signs of injury or arthritis should be watched for.

COAT TYPES

A low-maintenance smooth coat.

A silky coat with feathering.

The non-shedding Poodle coat.

A harsh-textured terrier coat.

VACCINATIONS

Chapter 2

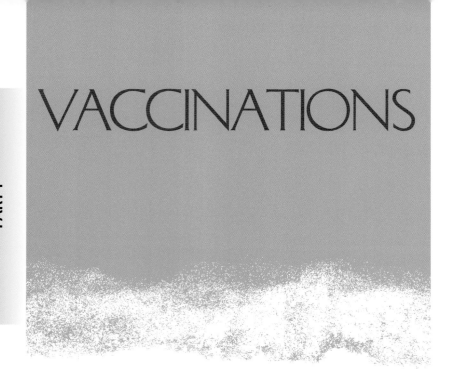

There can be no excuse for not providing the young puppy with protection against killer diseases. The puppy can be vaccinated as young as six weeks of age, but you must be advised by your own veterinary surgeon as to when the puppy should be receiving this protection. Often it will be at eight weeks for the first health check and initial vaccination, and then a second visit, probably between 10 and 12 weeks, to complete the protection for the first year.

Protection will be needed for the following:

PARVOVIRUS
This virus was a real killer of young dogs, who had no protection when this new disease appeared 25 years ago, causing dysentery and death from fluid loss and shock. Now newborn puppies are protected through their mothers but become susceptible to the illness as this maternal immunity wears off. Now if they meet the virus at 8 to 10 weeks, only 10 per cent of such infected puppies will die and most will recover after an illness of vomiting followed by diarrhoea.

Early vaccination is advised but because some bitches have high parvovirus antibody levels and pass on this immunity to the pups, it means that a second vaccine is necessary at 12 weeks.

CANINE DISTEMPER
A virus disease well known by older dog breeders, canine distemper can affect dogs of all ages. As well as severe catarrhal

Puppies receive initial immunity from their mother's milk.

disease signs, it can damage the nerves, previously being the most common cause of dog fits. Fortunately, due to decades of vaccination, the virus rarely appears now to do any harm. Distemper is still seen from time to time in unvaccinated dogs that have been allowed to wander in town areas. Epidemics may then occur among country pets and farmers' dogs where vaccination has been forgotten about and a stray dog is brought along for a country home. Pups can be protected by giving distemper vaccine as early as six weeks, but it is usual to follow your own veterinary surgeon's advice, as he will know the best times from his knowledge of your locality.

INFECTIOUS CANINE HEPATITIS

Canine adenovirus type 1 infection can cause a serious liver disease; fortunately, it is now rare but can still cause death from damaged blood vessels in young unvaccinated dogs. Dogs that recover may remain as carriers since the virus persists in the kidneys and is excreted in the urine. Collapse and death may be so fast in dogs that have sniffed or licked at such urine that poisoning is suspected: adenovirus in its severest form causes an illness lasting only 24 hours before death ensues.

A puppy needs to start a course of vaccinations when he arrives in his new home.

Infectious diseases spread rapidly in the dog population.

A terrier suffering from parvovirus on an intravenous drip. This is a common treatment for fluid loss.

The booster injection gives the vet a chance to give your dog a routine check-up.

LEPTOSPIROSIS

Unlike the previous three described, this disease is caused by bacteria, a type called spirochaetes that live outside the body in watercourses or in pools of urine left on the ground. Gundogs and any dogs that enjoy swimming in ponds and ditches are most at risk. The incubation is about seven days (4 to 12) after exposure. Leptospira cause a disease in humans called Weil's Disease. Dog vaccines now include the two types of bacteria that affect the kidneys and liver. Two doses of killed inactivated vaccine are given to produce immunity and for this disease it is necessary to give an annual 'booster' vaccine to keep up the protection.

KENNEL COUGH

Contrasting with the previous diseases that vaccination is advised for, this is not a 'killer', but infection causes a troublesome cough often lasting six weeks or more. There are several agents that can cause this type of cough and vaccines produced can contain one or several components. The most important elements are thought to be the bacteria *Bordetella bronchiseptica* and canine parainfluenza virus. Mycoplasma also complicate the infection and may account for slowness in effecting a cure for the cough. Vaccines are often used only at a time a few weeks before kennelling so as to provide the strongest immunity. A vaccine administered as one drop up the nose is not distressing to the dog and causes little discomfort. See also p. 85.

RABIES

It is necessary to use rabies vaccine at least six months before a dog is taken abroad. Vaccine can be given at three months of age and may require boosters every one to three years. Again, consult your vet if you think you may want to holiday abroad with your dog or if you live in a country where there is a risk. When travelling with your dog, be sure to carry the rabies vaccination certificate signed by a veterinarian or your pet's current rabies tag. A puppy suffering from rabies while in quarantine kennels in England bit staff working with dogs in 2008, so vigilance is needed even in safe countries.

BOOSTER VACCINES

The need for repeating the puppy vaccinations, known as booster vaccines, should be discussed with the veterinary surgeon. Booster vaccinations are needed when a dog's level of immunity has declined to a level where it no longer fully protects. Many of the virus type of vaccines protect for more than a year, so licensed manufacturers have changed to advising a repeat dose after three years. One vaccine manufacturer states their vaccine will give at least four years' protection against the 'core D, A, P viruses' (distemper, adeno and parvo viruses). For some diseases, such as leptospirosis, the vaccine must be given every 12 months to ensure protection.

VACCINATION CONCERNS

Following doubts about the use of the triple MMR vaccine in children with suggested possible injury to the brain, it was not unexpected that similar doubts arose about the need to give vaccines to young puppies. Seven components go into some dog vaccines and adjuvants may also be used for the injection the puppy will receive. There had been some reports of vague ill health in the weeks after vaccine had been injected. Dogs that developed fits (for one of many reasons, including hereditary epilepsy) caused distress to their new owners, and, in some cases, it brought back doubts about whether a vaccine could cause a brain injury. In 2004 an extensive survey was conducted by independent epidemiologists to look for an association between ill health in dogs following vaccination. The report in the prestigious journal *Vaccine* covered over 4,000 postal reports from owners of vaccinated dogs. The survey covered all dogs that had attended veterinary surgeries within the previous year and it was not surprising that a few had shown a mild reaction to a vaccination. Of those who responded to the questionnaire by filling it in, 23% of all the dogs had been recently vaccinated and only 1% of the dogs had not received a vaccine. From a statistical analysis of all the results, it was shown that recent vaccination did not increase ill health by more than 0.5% and may have decreased ill health of all the dogs by as much as 5%.

In the British Isles, distemper, parvovirus and leptospirosis are not the killer diseases of dogs

that they were 25 years ago. When veterinary nurses and even veterinary students are training it is difficult for them to observe the misery of a dog with a disease such as distemper, as it has become so rare. There is little likelihood that these three diseases will ever disappear entirely; the success story of mass vaccination of puppies with regular adult boosters can easily be forgotten. It is easier to forget the success of preventive measures and focus on a few unexplained illnesses that may or may not be associated with a recent vaccine given. Vaccination is safe for dogs.

The situation is not so clear when it comes to long delayed or chronic responses, such as skin conditions. A vaccine is intended to stimulate the dog's immune system and there may be individuals where the body 'overreacts'. The case for annual boosting of vaccines is now not so strong since this problem was suggested.

The worries of pet owners for the safe use of vaccine and the need to repeat these injections every year are based on a perceived risk rather than evidence-based fears. The financial cost of revaccination too has been another factor to make pet owners delay or hold back from further boosters. There has been a move to modify the revaccination schedules, as not every disease needs to be protected against by a vaccine given 12 monthly. This can lead to a less costly annual booster and it is always best to enquire from your vet what protection is being given, since distemper immunity lasts a longer time than, say, with protection against Leptospira where a killed vaccine is used.

PARASITES

Chapter 3

Parasites that live in or on the dog can cause concern. In extreme cases, they can cause the death of a dog and in several instances can be the cause of human ill health. A proper understanding of the risks and necessary preventive measures can keep the dog healthy and overcome objections to dogs associating with children or entering kitchens and food preparation areas.

Puppies should be treated routinely for roundworm infestation.

INTERNAL PARASITES

- The roundworm is probably the most frequent disquieting internal parasite. Such worms cause irritation in the intestines, and, in the puppy, they can cause lung and eye damage; a tangle of worms in the intestine could produce an obstruction and kill a pup. If vomited up, the worms can appear frighteningly evil. Roundworm eggs passed into the environment may also affect humans, causing disease.
- Tapeworms can be acquired by young or old dogs, but they cause less disastrous effects.
- Parasites such as *Giardia* can also cause severe diarrhoea and debility.
- Hookworms in some countries cause anaemia and severe illness but are still uncommon in the UK.
- The heartworm, spread by mosquito bites, may cause severe illness and death in countries outside the UK. Pets taken to mainland Europe may return carrying immature worms known as microfilariae. Infection results from the insect bite, and the worms (when adult) live inside the dog's heart.
- The lungworm or French heartworm *A. vasorum* is found where dogs eat slugs or snails.
- Whipworms, tracheal worms, bladder worms and other parasites may be found in puppies if samples are examined.

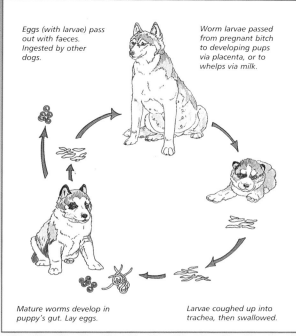

Eggs (with larvae) pass out with faeces. Ingested by other dogs.

Worm larvae passed from pregnant bitch to developing pups via placenta, or to whelps via milk.

Mature worms develop in puppy's gut. Lay eggs.

Larvae coughed up into trachea, then swallowed.

Roundworm lifecycle.

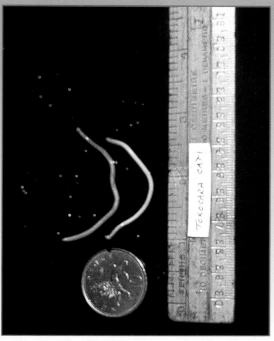

Roundworm – *Toxocara cati*. The coin gives an indication of size.

Veterinary advice on the risk of all internal parasites is important, and regular medication may be needed for prevention.

ROUNDWORMS

The two sorts of roundworm – Toxocara and Toxascaris – are similar enough to deal with together. Newborn puppies may carry worms of this sort acquired before birth from their mother. Toxocara larvae pass into puppies about the 42nd day of pregnancy.

SIGNS

- Puppies with a heavy worm infestation will be subject to diarrhoea and grow slowly.
- Pups will appear abnormally hungry, and never satisfied.

- If a pup is sick, one or more white coloured worm will appear in the vomit.
- The abdomen is unnaturally distended even long after a meal has been eaten.
- The dog's coat may be poor and lacking in shine following a worm infestation.
- Hiccups are not necessarily a sign of worms – all young creatures that have difficulty in controlling their breathing may be subject to such hiccups. Most adult dogs shed these worms, but if a bitch becomes pregnant, the encysted larval worms become active and migrate to the milk gland area and the placenta around the unborn puppies.

TREATMENT

About one in 10 adult dogs carry a few roundworms, so a regular worming routine for dogs throughout life with a combined round and tapeworm dose is recommended. Intervals of three or six months for worming are advised depending on the risk in your area. Adult dogs confined to their house and garden may have no need for such frequent worming, but a veterinary surgeon who knows the risk in the locality from the various worms would offer the best advice.

Unwormed puppies are the biggest producers of the worm eggs dangerous to children, so preventive treatment, which

PART I

entails the early worming of all puppies, is vital. Dosing should be repeated on a regular basis to stop the worms in a puppy getting to a size where more eggs will be laid. When children play in the same area as where dogs visit, the risks are increased.

There are many safe wormers obtained from veterinary suppliers. In the UK, there is a safe antibiotic-type wormer – selamectin or the newer combination of imidacloprid with moxidectin – used as a spot of liquid on the back of the neck once a month. Lufenuron and milbemycin is another combination treatment used once a month. Liquid wormers can be given to puppies every two weeks from 14 days old so the puppy on purchase at six or seven weeks should not have a problem. The bitch should be treated at the same time.

The new keeper of the puppy should aim to give a reliable wormer every three weeks between nine weeks and four months of age. Subsequently, worm the pup at six months and at 12 months. At this age it may then be advisable to use a combined roundworm/tapeworm tablet.

Worming the pregnant bitch from the 42nd day of her

Precautions should be taken when young children play with puppies.

pregnancy with a wormer such as Fenbendazole until 14 days after whelping is the best chance of producing a worm-free puppy to send out to a new home later.

PRECAUTIONS FOR CHILDREN WITH PETS

- Young children handling puppies should be told not to suck their fingers after touching them.
- Children who have been handling puppies or older dogs should be made to wash their hands before eating any food.
- The prompt removal of dog faeces from the ground and the use of designated toilet

areas for dogs – well away from children's play areas – is essential.

- Worm eggs passed out of the dog on to the ground will remain for up to a year as a source of infection to others. Worm eggs on the ground need from a few weeks in summer to several months in the winter before they become infective. Therefore, cleaning up after a dog defecates and depositing the product in a plastic bag in a bin helps to keep areas safe for children to play on.

TAPEWORMS

Tapeworms are more likely to be a problem in the dog over six months of age than in the younger dog. The main source of infection to a puppy with the Dipylidium tapeworm is from the flea or the biting louse. An infection could develop within weeks of the dog swallowing a flea on its coat, as the flea is the tapeworm's intermediate host.

There are several types of Taenia tapeworms that affect dogs. *Diphyllobothrium* species, which are found encysted in fish, can affect dogs. The most dangerous worm to humans – Echinococcus – is now fortunately rare but can cause trouble when dogs scavenge sheep offal.

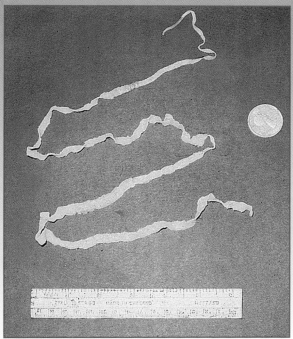

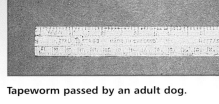

Tapeworm passed by an adult dog.

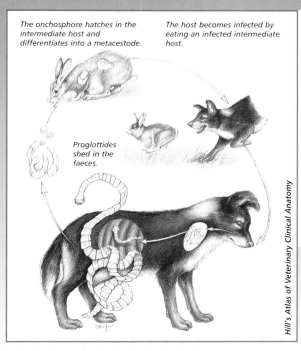

The onchosphore hatches in the intermediate host and differentiates into a metacestode.

The host becomes infected by eating an infected intermediate host.

Proglottides shed in the faeces.

Hill's Atlas of Veterinary Clinical Anatomy

Tapeworm lifecycle.

SIGNS

The tapeworm segments look like flattened grains of rice and are seen on freshly voided faeces or sometimes stuck on to tail hairs around the anus.

TREATMENT

Routine worming at six months with an effective tapeworm tablets is advised as well as flea control. Some of the worming products can be given any time of day on an empty stomach. Others specify that the tablets be given in the morning with a small breakfast meal then the rest of the food is given five hours later.

Usually no signs of the worms are seen after dosing, as they are dissolved away once killed as part of the dog's digestive process. It is also necessary to remember the more deadly tapeworm, Echinococcus, is a danger to dogs and humans. It is only found in two small areas on the British Isles where dogs have access to dead sheep. A related Echinococcus is found in Europe, passing through rats to infect dogs, foxes and cats. There are other tapeworms that have the rabbit as an intermediate host. Infected raw beef, sheep or pig meat used to carry cysts of tapeworms in the past; there is

also an Echinococcus that has a horse flesh to dog life cycle, but this meat is not fed raw to dogs in the UK.

HOOKWORMS (ANCYLOSTOMA & UNCINARIA)

The name is given because, under the magnifying lens, the hookworm has tiny hooks on its head. Hookworms burrow into the wall of the large intestine to feed and cause more damage than roundworms.

SIGNS

The signs to look for are blood-

23

PART I

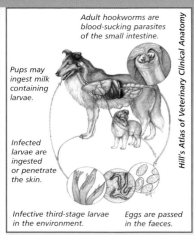

Adult hookworms are blood-sucking parasites of the small intestine.

Pups may ingest milk containing larvae.

Infected larvae are ingested or penetrate the skin.

Infective third-stage larvae in the environment.

Eggs are passed in the faeces.

Hill's Atlas of Veterinary Clinical Anatomy

Hookworm lifecycle.

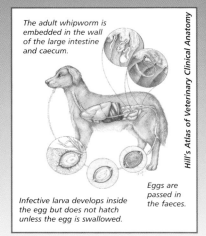

The adult whipworm is embedded in the wall of the large intestine and caecum.

Infective larva develops inside the egg but does not hatch unless the egg is swallowed.

Eggs are passed in the faeces.

Hill's Atlas of Veterinary Clinical Anatomy

Whipworm lifecycle.

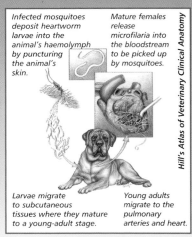

Infected mosquitoes deposit heartworm larvae into the animal's haemolymph by puncturing the animal's skin.

Mature females release microfilaria into the bloodstream to be picked up by mosquitoes.

Larvae migrate to subcutaneous tissues where they mature to a young-adult stage.

Young adults migrate to the pulmonary arteries and heart.

Hill's Atlas of Veterinary Clinical Anatomy

Heartworm lifecycle.

stained diarrhoea, which will eventually result in an anaemic, thin dog. The worm larvae of Uncinaria can burrow into the dog's skin, causing a dermatitis.

Eggs are not produced every day by the worm, so it may be necessary to take faeces samples for several days before the characteristic thick-walled eggs are seen under the microscope. Eggs of this worm remain in the soil for a year or more, so a dog that eats grass or buries bones in infected soil is the one most likely to have these worms. Most of the wormers used have the ability to kill whipworms. However, the common wormer Piperazine needs to be given at the double dose of 200mg/kg by mouth in order to be effective.

WHIPWORM

This is a small worm, 2-3 in (6 cm) in length, but it has a whip-like appearance under the microscope. It burrows into the mucous membrane of the large intestine and will cause bloody, mucus-filled diarrhoea. It is associated with hounds and dogs using permanent grass runs – but is rare in the UK. Exercise runs should be concreted and treated with bleach regularly if a problem occurs.

BLADDER AND LIVER WORMS

Capillaria plica is known as the bladder worm. Again, it is rare in the UK but eggs are passed in the urine of affected dogs. Specimens can be examined in the laboratory: worming with an effective drug will then be needed. Another type of Capillaria lives in rats and could cause infection if a dog catches and eats a rat.

HEART AND LUNG WORMS

Lungworms do not really occur except those found in the blood vessels of the lungs when the signs include coughing and difficulty in breathing. Dogs may catch the *Angiostrongylus vasorum* worm after eating a snail containing the infective larvae. Foxes, frogs and snails also carry the worm. The spread of this infection in England was confined to the south-west and south Wales, but it is now being seen in northern parts of England as well. It is sometimes called the 'French heartworm'.

The adult worms live in the artery, passing through the lung of the dog. The adult females produce eggs that travel to the lung alveoli, hatch and the larvae then emerge through the alveolar walls, to be coughed up, swallowed and passed to the outside in the faeces.

Clinically, the most dangerous is the heartworm *Dirofilaria immitis*, which is not usually found in the UK but is a major problem in America and many other countries, so it may be found after dogs are imported into England. The worm lives within the heart and the immature larvae can be found in blood smears. If an insect such as a mosquito feeds, it transfers the microfilariae from one dog to another. Sudden death from heart failure can result if the condition is not recognised.

Various preventive treatments given daily or monthly depending on the product used, following veterinary instructions. Elderly dogs with heartworm may have a high risk of dying if treatment is given to eliminate worms already in the heart. Veterinary advice should be taken and closely followed.

The tracheal worm *Oslerus osleri* was named after a Canadian physician who studied comparative medicine in people and animals. The adult worms live in small nodules at the base of the trachea or windpipe. The worm's nodules can only be seen on passing an endoscope tube down towards the lungs, so may easily be overlooked. Adult worms produce eggs that are coughed up and swallowed. Any coughing dog – Greyhounds especially – may be carrying this worm. Dog-to-dog infection after coughing is possible, or a bitch may infect her pups as she licks them.

Flukes are flat worms that can get into the lungs of dogs. In the US, lung flukes may be found in dogs who live near to water or have access to low-lying wet areas. Worming, as advised by your vet, is effective. Any further infection by swallowing aquatic snails and crayfish should be prevented. Other sorts of liver fluke occur in wet fields in England, but they only affect sheep.

WORMING: IS IT NECESSARY?

The advice must be to worm every three to six months whether you see worms in your dog or not. Where there is any unusual diarrhoea or illness, your veterinary surgeon may ask for a faecal sample to analyse under the microscope. This can be obtained in the following way:

- Use a plastic lid as a scoop for recently voided faeces
- Place in a small bottle. Fill it up, keep air out as far as possible and seal it
- Deliver it to the veterinary practice
- Don't forget to label it with details that include the dog's age as well as other identifications.

Some flea preparations applied to the skin every month will protect the dog against some of the worms internally. If in doubt, you should ask for veterinary advice from a practitioner who knows the problem in the locality.

EXTERNAL PARASITES

Any dog may be seen to scratch himself occasionally and even roll on his back to relieve some mild itch. However, if the dog has a good healthy coat, which is not dry and scurfy, an occasional scratch of the body from the back leg is not unexpected.

A patchy coat with bare areas of hair loss, scaly skin and persistent scratching may well indicate a parasitic skin disease.

- The most frequently encountered insect living in the coat of the puppy is the flea.
- There are many other parasites that may be found on the skin, ranging from the clearly visible dog tick to the mite.
- Cheyletiella only recognised as 'walking dandruff'. A black dog can have white skin scales visible on the coat surface; if some of these may be seen to move if closely observed in a bright light, then a parasite is the cause.
- Itchy skins and white eggs or 'nits' stuck to the hairs will suggest one of several types of body lice as a cause.
- There are the burrowing mites that invade the hair follicles and the skin thickness: Demodex and Sarcoptes are the most frequently encountered.
- Mites also live in the outer ear canal. The Otodectes surface mite can cause intense ear irritation and a cat in the family is often the source of infection.
- Ringworm as a mycosis or skin fungus infection may affect some dogs but this is usually a rare occurrence.

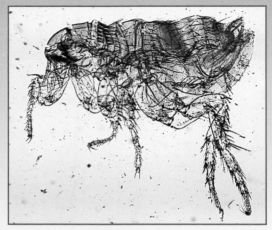

The dog flea *Ctenocephalides canis*.

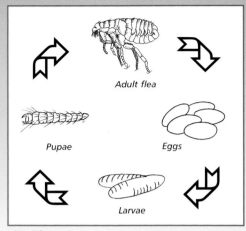

Flea life cycle.

The fleas and lice on the dog prefer the taste of dog's blood and skin to the human equivalent, so do not think all these parasites will nibble or bite humans. When hungry, the flea will bite humans. The bites will only be recognised later by an intense itching, minutes or hours after the flea has bitten the person's body. The same can be said of Cheyletiella, as it is often the person's itchy skin that first draws the dog owner's attention to this parasite living on the dog's coat.

FLEAS

In recent years the flea has benefited from a warmer climate in Europe and North America and an increase in the domestic cat population. In the UK, hedgehogs are often found in gardens, so dogs exploring under leaf heaps are at risk. This contact, especially when the hedgehog is hibernating, can bring in the hedgehog's own type of fleas to live on dogs. Foxes may also carry fleas and when entering gardens may deposit skin parasites – which the dog picks up when rolling in fox mess.

Fleas like a warm, humid environment. Eggs can hatch in 10 days, although they could remain dormant for a year if the weather is dry or cold. Outdoor control of fleas may involve disinfecting yards, runs or any regular resting areas, such as dry grass. Small wild animals should be discouraged from coming to these areas, as they could bring in more flea eggs.

Cats seem to tolerate a few fleas living on their body and the remains of flea feeding activities may only be recognised as black 'crumbs' or a gritty substance lying close to the cat's skin. The cat flea can then move on to a dog where the flea is more likely to cause intense irritation after it has punctured the skin and sucked some of the blood.

SIGNS

The signs of fleas are not always obvious. They may be recognised by a patch of thin undercoat, a few broken hairs and some brown scales on the skin surface. Excessive nibbling, licking and grooming with the teeth are signs of the itching from a flea bite; there may be short broken hairs as well as signs of hair loss. Another clue may be the dampness of the hair where the dog has excessively groomed in an attempt to catch the flea.

Inspect the dog's skin by parting the hairs to see down to the skin level, then look for live brown fleas running through the coat. You may find the black flecks that are the flea dirt or excreta. A very bright light helps to find fleas and often the heat of the lamp makes the fleas more active and easier to see when they move across the skin. If black flea crumbs are found, brush them on to a white surface, such as clean paper. If the paper is then moistened, the black crumbs become reddish-brown on the white background. The flea dirt still contains some dried blood, which accounts for the colour change on moistening with water.

FURTHER FLEA RISKS

A young dog with a heavy flea infestation may become anaemic, which is a direct result of the amount of blood lost by parasites feeding on blood. The female fleas feed for longer than the male flea, as they need an extra food supply to lay many eggs. Systemic flea preparations, such as the monthly tablets, are more likely to kill off the female fleas that spend longer feeding from the dog. Male fleas usually only need a short feed after one bite and they then leave the dog's skin to wait elsewhere. A spray with a quick-kill component may be the best way of ridding the body of both sorts of fleas.

A further risk to the puppy is that some fleas contain the tapeworm intermediate stage (see p. 22).

FLEA BITE ALLERGY

Allergy to flea bites and irritants in the flea saliva can produce

JUMPING FLEAS

Released fleas jump to magnetic north and so fleas were highly valued when they were used to help the navigators of Viking long ships.

long-lasting itching and scratching even when all the fleas have apparently been removed from the dog. The first flea bite may commence the allergic response known as 'hypersensitivity'. The next time the flea bites, a reaction occurs in 12 to 24 hours with a papular skin reaction and redness. Later on, there is an immediate reaction to the flea bites (within an hour), with itching, redness and swelling; this means that antibodies (IgE) and cytotoxic antibodies have been produced during sensitisation to bites. One flea is all that is necessary to produce this reaction. Fleas are one of the commonest causes of long-lasting skin disease in adult dogs.

LIFE CYCLE
- Each female flea lays at least 150 eggs. All these eggs fall off the dog or cat, 60 per cent within two hours of being

deposited.
- The eggs hatch on the ground or in carpets in two to 10 days depending on temperature. The eggs are barely visible to the human eye. They are oval in shape, a pearly white colour about 0.5 mm long.
- Once the eggs hatch, the larvae live away from the dog host. They are creamy yellow, 2-5 mm long, and very rarely seen.
- The larvae have to pass through two moults to develop. A flea larva can lie dormant for up to a year if no host is present for the adult flea to feed from. In a cold and dry house, the larva or pupa can lie in wait until an animal or human passes through. A human footfall from across an empty room will attract many fleas to a person when a house has been left unoccupied for months.

TREATMENT

There are numerous preparations now available for flea control and the most appropriate product to use can be advised by the veterinary surgeon or nurse. Some products should not be used until the puppy is three months old. The young puppy (after veterinary advice) can be sprayed with Fipronil from two days of age and this is the only safe method for the tiniest puppy that comes with fleas. Bathing with a shampoo will not necessarily kill all the fleas but they will then show up in the wet coat or many may be washed off in the rinse water.

Live fleas need squashing with a finger nail or similar since their hard-shelled flattened bodies withstand normal thumb pressure on a hard surface. Drowning eventually kills fleas, but they swim for some time and will still be able to hop away if allowed to dry out!

- **Spot-on treatments:** These are applied easily to the skin halfway down the neck. The drug blocks the insect's GABA receptors, thus killing fleas and lice on contact. The place of application is important, as the puppy should not be able to lick it. Although considered safe, normally Fiprinol should not be used on puppies under 8 weeks of age. Selamectin can be used on puppies aged 10 weeks or more, and is unique in also controlling roundworms internally. Repeat treatment with spot-ons are needed monthly in the flea season.
- **Aerosol spray:** Aerosol sprays of insecticides can also be used from as early as 7 to 12 weeks of age, but only in a two-second burst. Repeated applications may be necessary and some animals become fearful of the hissing sound that many sprays make.
- **Flea collar:** A flea collar can be placed around the dog's neck. The collar is treated with chemicals against fleas, but

Spot-on treatment is an effective measure and is easy to apply.

they are often less effective, as the fleas prefer the rump area to feed rather than the neck regions of the dog.

- **Growth regulator:** A further method of control is the flea growth regulator 'Lufenuron', which stops the pupa developing into an adult flea; it blocks the formation of a hard chitin layer in the larva as it develops. Insecticides that kill adult fleas will be necessary if there is a heavy initial flea infestation, but any fleas on the treated animal depositing eggs in the house will not be able to reinfect other animals. There is the risk with this method that other dogs or visiting cats may drop flea eggs around the house that are not inhibited from turning into adult biting fleas. A combination of Fiprinol with s-methoprene (Frontline Combo) kills fleas on the dog

and prevents the development of flea eggs, larvae, and pupae in the environment and is recommended as a spot-on. It is called a non-systemic parasiticide and some consider it safer.

IN THE HOUSE

Once a dog has come into the home carrying a flea, a necessary part of flea control is to treat the floors, carpets and furnishings used by that dog. This is known as environmental control, as any surface may have flea eggs dropped on to it. Then, after hatching, larvae spin a sticky cocoon with bits of fluff, and dirt sticks to them as a source of food and protection. There are a number of environmental sprays to kill larvae and they can last for between three and 12 months.

The use of a vacuum cleaner is beneficial in removing flea debris, but the cleaner needs emptying in an outdoor bin to stop an adult flea developing from the pupa in the bag. Furniture should be moved and carpet edges treated, as larvae migrate into the depth of the fabric and often away from light, so deep-pile carpets can be a particular problem.

Foggers, used in the USA, produce a mist that settles on carpets, but not in all the deep crevices. High-residue levels may be a problem – children especially should be kept out of treated areas.

NATURAL PARASITE REMEDIES

Some dog owners prefer to use naturally occurring products to control fleas. The most effective of those available is pyrethrum from poppies. Pyrethroid, which is manufactured to mimic the natural pyrethrum, is an effective flea killer and can be purchased as a dusting powders. Generally speaking, powders do not get deep enough into the coat of longer-haired dogs to be fully effective. Baths containing pyrethroids are then the most effective way to apply the product.

Garlic in the food has been praised by some breeders as a way of keeping their dogs entirely free of fleas. Other essential oils, such as lavender used on the coat, have some repellent action. In former times, dogs were kennelled on shredded pine wood used as bedding and fleas were unknown. Cedar or eucalyptus wood shavings can sometimes be used for the same purpose. Eucalyptus oil and pennyroyal can be poisonous to a young dog if licked off the coat and should not be used.

LICE

As a prehistoric parasite, lice have been identified in archaeological remains. They are often associated with bad living conditions and with close animal-to-animal contact. Lice can be carriers of other diseases, such as

A dog may need repeated applications of flea spray.

human typhus – one of the scourges of the medieval world.

SIGNS

The eggs of lice stick to dog hair and can be seen as tiny white objects (nits) glued to the hair. The ear fringes are a good place to check. Clipping the ear fringes short and paying attention to the area at the front of the elbows can also help to remove lice.

There are two sorts of lice affecting dogs: the surface feeders that bite are probably easier to remove; the burrowing type that suck are the more difficult to eliminate. The sucking lice can cause anaemia from blood loss, but the first effect noticed is an intense irritation.

TREATMENT

Treatment with antiparasitic washes were advised, but now many of the flea treatments described previously work equally well against lice.

TICKS

Ticks are much bigger in size than either fleas or lice. In the UK, the most common ticks are those that come from sheep and those that come from hedgehogs. They are different in size and colour and they can be identified at a veterinary clinic if you capture them in a bottle.

By far the commonest tick seen in the UK is the sheep tick *Ixodes ricinus* – a particular problem for country dogs. The hedgehog tick, *Ixodes hexagonus*, may be more common in town areas where there are large gardens. Deer ticks occur in Scotland; in the USA the female wood tick bite produces tick paralysis. The signs of illness appear about a week after the tick bite; the paralysis develops slowly and death from respiratory arrest may occur.

SIGNS

The owner of a dog carrying a tick is more likely to think it is a wart growing on the animal's head or body than it is an insect sucking blood. Sometimes multiple tick infestations occur and many pin-head sized ticks will be found at various places on the body.

Always examine your dog after coming back from exercise on moorland or in woodland or long grass: prompt removal of visible ticks will stop them feeding and introducing disease. The female tick takes a blood meal five to 24 hours after arriving on the dog.

The dog, as the 'host', will allow the tick to swell as it engorges the blood.

LIFE CYCLE

The tick is an eight-legged insect that attaches itself by very strong 'teeth' or mouthparts to the dog's skin and it then proceeds to suck blood. As the tick feeds, its reddish-brown body becomes more bloated and slate grey as it fills with blood. Eventually the tick drops off as a fully fed adult.

The female tick then deposits thousands of eggs on the ground, which hatch and turn into larvae, awaiting the arrival of another animal to feed from. Any ticks found on the body should be removed as soon as possible – before they have sucked too much blood and before they are ready to lay thousands of eggs on the ground.

FURTHER RISKS

As well as causing anaemia, the tick can be a vector or carrier of serious life-threatening disease. Lyme disease is a major problem in some areas of the United States and occurs from time to time in the UK. Find out from your veterinary surgeon if it is a problem in your area. There is a Lyme disease vaccine available. There are other tick fevers that are a problem in many countries, such as Rocky Mountain Spotted

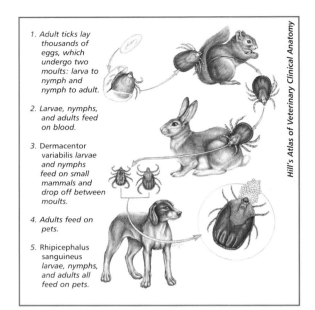

1. Adult ticks lay thousands of eggs, which undergo two moults: larva to nymph and nymph to adult.

2. Larvae, nymphs, and adults feed on blood.

3. Dermacentor variabilis larvae and nymphs feed on small mammals and drop off between moults.

4. Adults feed on pets.

5. Rhipicephalus sanguineus larvae, nymphs, and adults all feed on pets.

Hill's Atlas of Veterinary Clinical Anatomy

Tick lifecycle.

Fever, canine babesiosis, canine ehrlichosis and canine hepatozoonosis, that were present for many years in the USA. Tick paralysis is a problem in Australia, too.

If you are in a locality where ticks are prevalent, it is necessary to inspect the dog every day during grooming time, to see if there are ticks about. This is especially the case in spring and summer. Small ticks should be looked for: the ears, the neck and under the fore legs should be closely searched for ticks.

Ticks may also carry the blood parasite Babesia, which, in central Europe, North America and elsewhere worldwide, can cause súdden collapse and death. The parasite destroys the blood cells, so red urine or haemoglobinuria

may be the first sign of Babesiosis.

The brown dog tick (*Rhipecephlus sanguineus*) is a blood sucking tick that is common in Mediterranean countries and some parts of the USA. It can be the cause of the blood and liver disease known as canine hepatozoonosis, which may be life-threatening. This is another example of the dangers involved when dogs are taken out of their own country for holiday or for other reasons. Treatment by aggressive tick control is essential; an acaracide with repellent activity, such as a spot-on containing both imidacloprid and permethrin, is advised to remove the tick parasite from attacking the dog's blood.

TREATMENT

Ticks should never be plucked off, as this will leave the hard mouthparts firmly embedded and the dog will later develop a hard nodule and a non-healing wound around the embedded part.

- Use tweezers or a plastic 'tick hook' to get close to the head.
- Gently pull with a slow twisting movement until the tick lets go.
- This procedure is made easier if the tick is first coated with olive oil or a mineral oil to block its breathing tubes. You can also use an oily ear mite preparation that contains an acaracide.

Rubbing the tick with nail varnish remover, alcohol or a commercial tick spray will also help to kill the tick before removing it.

- When removing the tick, take care not to squeeze its abdomen, as this can lead to the stomach contents being regurgitated into the dog's bloodstream, increasing the likelihood of infection.
- It may be wise to give an antibiotic soon after the tick has been removed to avoid any blood poisoning.

EAR MITES

These parasites only live inside the ear canal but they can be a problem. The parasite Otodectes is usually caught from a cat. Close contact with the cat is not necessary, as a cat shaking its head may propel pieces of wax containing mites, which fly through the air and can arrive on the dog's coat.

SIGNS

Even one or two mites in the ear produce redness and intense irritation. If a dog scratches at his ear with his back toenails, scratch wounds may be found in the ear and bacteria will then infect this

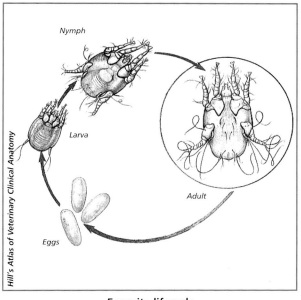

Hill's Atlas of Veterinary Clinical Anatomy

Nymph

Larva

Eggs

Adult

Ear mite lifecycle.

warm moist red ear area with severe consequences.

TREATMENT

Daily treatment using an acaracide for a week will be needed to get rid of ear mites. Cats in contact must also be treated to reduce the risk of reinfection.

OTHER 'BUGS'

- Minor skin disorders may be seen on bare areas of skin as round spots with a pink 'ring' around them. These are not necessarily ringworm (see p. 121) and may be a bacterial Staphylococcus toxin response in young dogs.
- The so-called 'hospital super

bug' has been prominent as a cause of death and infection in human hospitals. It is a special Staphylococcus that has become resistant to the antibiotic methcillin and to nearly every other antibiotic in use. Although not normally a cause of death in canine patients after operations, routine swab testing has recently shown that a few dogs may carry these 'super bugs' in their nose and throat or on their skin. Most have been associated in dogs that have owners who work in a human hospital environment or with immunosuppressed people for some reason. Any dog from such a family that has a persisting sore throat or skin spots with a pink 'ring' around them may be a bacterial carrier of Staphylcoccus and swab tests are advised.

All vets are aware that MRSA, although not common, is a risk in veterinary practice. Many members of the public have been exposed to infection and some are carriers of the bacteria. Vets will be on the look out for non-healing wounds and intransient infections. Steps may be taken to test staff who have handled such wound infections, but hygiene and cleanliness are important.

FIRST-AID

Chapter

ost emergencies affecting your dog require a common sense approach: keep calm and try to avoid a panic reaction. Take time to assess the situation and decide whether a trip to the vet is immediately necessary. Many minor injuries can be dealt with by a calm, knowledgeable owner armed with a good first-aid kit, though it goes without saying that, if in doubt, a vet should be called.

WHEN YOU SHOULD CALL THE VET

A little blood from an ear tip wound or a cut pad can look like a life-threatening emergency when you first see the amount of blood smeared on the walls or walked all over a light-coloured floor.

With such types of bleeding, it is important to try to apply a 'compress' to staunch the blood flow. Applying a pressure pad, such as a damp tea towel, may be the first thing you can reach for. This will help immediately, but then try to get some form of 'pressure bandage' on as the first-aid treatment, and then assess the amount of blood being lost.

The Dobermann Pinscher I treated that put his head through a glass door on the eve of a general election in response to a canvasser of votes required more specific first-aid. The dog's neck was badly cut almost down to the neck arteries, but a sensible visitor in the house was able to wrap a towel round the neck and cuddled the dog beside them to keep a firm pressure on the wound area. When the vet arrived (it was some distance from his surgery), the dog was examined for the colour of his gums, the dog's blood pressure was taken, and then a strong

sedative was given before applying stitches to the cut neck to stop blood flow from the gaping wound. The dog could then be taken to the main veterinary surgery for intravenous fluids for shock and for more accurate wound stitching. But without the visitor's first-aid and calm approach, the dog would have died.

HOW TO RECOGNISE AN EMERGENCY

The four most common emergencies with dogs are:
• Sudden pain
• Bleeding wounds
• Fractured limbs or spine
• Severe diarrhoea

First-aid measures can be divided into simple procedures that you can use at home and more essential actions, such as for the dog involved in a road traffic accident, who will have to get to a veterinary hospital with as little delay as possible but who needs some treatment 'on the spot'.

URGENT CASES

- Acute dysentery, bloody diarrhoea
- Repeated and persistent vomiting
- Choking, any swelling in the face or neck regions
- Collapse or sudden loss of consciousness
- Deep or long skin wounds
- Fits that are unduly prolonged or repeated
- Ingestion of rat or herbicide poisons or human medications
- Profuse bleeding that cannot be stopped
- Road traffic accidents
- Sudden swellings: an eyeball and protrusion, a distended abdomen or a lip or leg swelling as after a snake bite
- An inability to walk or to use the back legs, or severe back pain

VETERINARY ADVICE IN EMERGENCIES

At present all veterinary surgeons in the UK are required to offer a 24-hour service. This is not the case in North America, where, in many cases, it will be necessary to find an 'out of hours' emergency clinic. In Britain there is a growing number of emergency clinics that specialise in 'out of hours' calls, which have considerable experience and equipment to deal with such events. It is best to contact the vet you have your dog registered with first, to find out where to go

The responsible owner should master the basics of first-aid care.

to obtain help. Sometimes a reassuring word will be given to turn a presumed emergency into a controllable dog situation that can be attended to later. The dog may need hospitalisation; he can be taken in for observation and measures such as drips and X-rays can be provided at the right location. The best advice is to call your own vet if you are in any doubt and follow his or her recommendations.

FIRST-AID MEASURES AT HOME

SICKNESS AND DIARRHOEA

Dogs that feel sick may often provoke vomiting by eating coarse grasses. The dog will empty his stomach contents as a survival mechanism relating to the primitive habit of food scavenging.

Mild cases of diarrhoea and sickness do not constitute an

Sickness and diarrhoea may result if a dog has been scavenging or stealing.

CALL THE VET

Seek veterinary care at the earliest opportunity for all but the smallest injuries. In the case of severe injury where the dog is suffering from shock, the vet will set up an intravenous fluid drip, which will help to correct any metabolic problem. By restoring blood volume and circulation, oxygen can be more easily conveyed to the brain and to vital tissues.

emergency and can be dealt with at home. First-aid measures include allowing the dog to drink very small quantities of ice-cold fluid, to combat dehydration, and to withhold all solid food for 24 hours. Start the dog on bland food, such as minced chicken and cooked rice, in small quantities. If the situation persists, then report the signs to your vet.

You should also call the vet if you think poison has been taken in. Repeated sickness and retching is often accompanied by panting and pawing at the mouth, followed by collapse. Secondary poisoning is where a dog eats a poisoned rat, rabbit or bird that has accumulated a lethal dose in its body before it died or was perhaps already weak and easily caught.

Acute diarrhoea with or without blood may be a sign of poisoning but it is more likely

due to a bacterial or virus infection. Fluid and blood lost may result in death due to shock from a collapse of the circulatory system. Warning signs in a dog include lying flat out on a cold floor, sunken eyes, rapid, weak pulse and cold extremities. Other signs of shock include pale mucous membranes and a slow capillary refill when the gums are pressed hard with the finger.

This simple test consists of pressing on the gums to blanch them and waiting for pink to reappear (one to two seconds is normal). This will indicate how serious the fluid loss is or whether shock may be developing. Any increase in capillary refill time may indicate shock but is also seen in dehydration, hypovolaemia (a fall in the volume of blood in the circulation) or hypotension. A decrease in the time is found with pain or with septic shock or fevers.

BLOATED STOMACH
Another emergency is gastric bloating where the dog attempts to vomit and becomes more and more distressed as the stomach fills with gas. It can be seen to bulge like a drum on the left side of the abdomen. Gastric bloating or 'tympany' requires immediate veterinary attention at a well-equipped clinic or hospital, as it is a life-threatening emergency.

CUTS AND WOUNDS
Wounds may be from dog bites, with bruising of the flesh, or clean cuts from glass or barbed wire.

Each situation requires different first-aid, but bathing with a weak salt solution and applying a compress to stem the flow of blood should be within the ability of the first-aider. For those wishing to use 'natural cures', calendula tea has been used as an effective wound

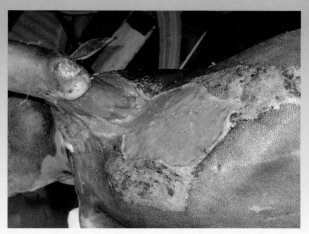

Crossbreed with extensive wounds and skin loss due to a wire fence injury.

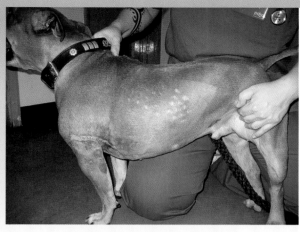

The same dog after his wounds have healed.

dressing. It should be applied cold and has the advantage that it does not mat up the hair, unlike greasy ointments. The tea is an infusion that must be made fresh each day; boiling water is poured on the dried calendula herb and then the infusion sieved off and allowed to cool.

Call the vet, as injuries often will need professional attention. Cuts may need stitching to bring the skin edges together, but infected wounds may need antibiotics and surface cleaning before later repair by stitching. Abrasions, when there is a loss of skin surface, may need prolonged dressing until skin repair can take place. Always consider that there is the risk of internal injuries.

BURNS AND SCALDS
Burns can be very painful and after a house fire there is the delayed complications of smoke inhalation. Dogs can also be burnt as a result of household accidents, such as being scalded by hot water from a kettle or hot fat from a pan.

Apply a stream of cold water for up to 15 minutes if the burn is to a leg or a part of the body that is accessible. The dog may need to be treated for shock, which involves making the animal comfortable and keeping the room warm so there is no further heat loss from the body. It may be possible to offer small quantities of fluid by mouth, but not if an anaesthetic at the vet's will later be required.

Call the vet if in doubt about such injuries.

ROAD TRAFFIC ACCIDENTS
In the event of a road traffic accident, you may have to restrain and secure the frightened dog. A dog that is in pain will turn round and bite the offered hand, even if it is the familiar owner or someone else the dog trusts.

If the dog looks frightened, then a loose tape muzzle applied around the mouth may help in calming as well as preventing biting, particularly if it is accompanied by reassuring, soothing words.

Great care should be taken when moving a dog that appears to have suffered broken bones or a dislocation. Broken legs are obvious by the distortion, but splinting is not generally advised. Dislocations of the hip or other joints are less painful, but the leg will be at an unusual angle compared with the opposite limb.

Often, it is better to leave the dog lying in the same place; as long as he will not receive further injuries, such as if he is left on the roadway. Some dogs will recover sufficiently after the initial shock of an accident to get up and carefully move themselves, minimising any pain. Forceful lifting may aggravate an injury, so great care should always be taken if trying to move a casualty. It may be possible to roll a dog on to an adjacent blanket or ease a similar cloth or sheet underneath a dog, so as to allow lifting from either end by two or more helpers. Veterinary ambulances will carry a stretcher, which is best for safely moving an injured dog.

If there is a possibility of a spinal fracture, it means sliding the dog on to a hard board before he is moved: this is to stop the spine kinking further and causing irreparable nerve damage and permanent paralysis. Call the vet or emergency clinic for advice before moving such a dog.

In all situations involving road

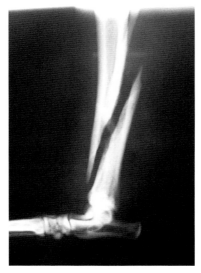

Fracture of bones in the hindleg after a road traffic accident. A successful repair was made.

traffic accidents, you must get the dog to the veterinary centre. Ask if there is an ambulance service. Even if the dog appears to have recovered, there is always the risk of internal injuries.

TAIL INJURIES

The tail can be trodden on easily; if a painful swelling results, the vertebra bone inside may have been broken. An unusual injury is found in dogs that go swimming: after entering the cold water they may be found to have a paralysed tail. This is thought to be due to the dog raising up the tail to act as a rudder, but, in so doing, causes pressure on nerves inside. Seen in gundogs that enter the water, recovery usually takes place in a few days.

ANAL GLAND PROBLEMS

Just under the tail are found a pair of 'glands' or anal sacs. These often become distended, cause pain or the dog may lick them frequently. If the infected sac bursts, there will be a discharge of blood fluid and the pain will go away. You may recognise the early anal sac signs by the dog tobogganing or 'scooting' along the carpet.

The competent first-aider can apply pressure around the anus in a 5 and 7 o'clock position; lifting the tail at the base also helps to empty the glands. Keep a good pad of cotton wool ready to catch the contents, as the sacs contain malodorous creamy fluid.

Call the vet when you do not have the experience to empty the anal glands.

DROWNING AND SUFFOCATION

Dogs are good swimmers so rarely lose their lives through drowning. However, exceptional circumstances may lead to the need for rescue and resuscitation. Such circumstances include the dog that falls into the swimming pool and cannot find his way out, or a dog in a lake that had been attacked by a swan guarding its nest, resulting in a blow from the bird's wing and possibly then being held under water.

First, get the dog out of the water and hold him upside down to try to drain water out of his mouth and throat. If the dog is unconscious, use your fingers to scoop out any weed at the back of the throat. Once you have cleared the airway, apply chest massage to try to pump air into the lungs. You can also apply your mouth to the dog's nostrils to try to force your exhaled breath into the lungs. Keep up the artificial respiration and massage around the heart through the rib cage.

Next, call the vet. You will need to get the dog to the vet with the greatest urgency so that oxygen can be given directly into the windpipe leading down to the lungs. See CPR below.

LOSS OF CONSCIOUSNESS, ELECTROCUTION

First assess the situation: if there is an electric supply in contact with the dog, switch the supply off before touching the dog or, at worst, pull the dog away with a long-handled dry wooden broomstick. Dogs that receive electric shock may also be burned, so look at the fur. Look at the dog's eyes – are they wide open or does the dog seem asleep? Are the pupils dilated? Is the breathing rate faster or slower than normal? Could there have been a head injury? Is there saliva around the mouth, suggesting a recent fit? Heat stroke is yet another possibility.

If the dog is unconscious, apply cardiopulmonary resuscitation (CPR). This procedure requires artificial respiration and heart massage.

STEPS IN RESUSCITATION:

First decide which basic life support will need to be used.
- Watch the dog's breathing: observe the rise and fall of the chest; feel for air being exhaled with the back of your hand or even your cheek.
- If breathing, pull out the tongue and clear anything from inside the mouth using fingers or a dry cloth. Obstructions must be removed, even sticky saliva.
- If not breathing, next look for the dog's pulse. Try to feel the femoral artery inside the back leg near the pelvis or feel for the dog's heart beat.
- If the dog has a pulse, start rescue breathing (artificial respiration).
- If the dog has no pulse, start cardiopulmonary resuscitation (CPR).

The dog is a natural swimmer, but he may struggle in hazardous circumstances.

CPR TECHNIQUE
This consists of artificial breathing together with heart massage.
- To begin, open the mouth, pull the tongue forward and hold it there.
- Check again for a pulse or heart beat. Heart massage can be done through the rib cage over the heart area.
- Chest compression on a small dog is best done using the flat of the two hands applied either side of the chest. Try for a compression rate around the heart of 100 a minute. The rate must be faster than that typically used in human artificial respiration, i.e. needs to mimic a natural panting type of breathing. Keep this going until the dog breathes on his own or as long as the heart beat remains.
- With a large dog, two people need to work together, one using the mouth-to-nose

breathing and the other using chest compression at about 80 to the minute. Firmer techniques are needed for the large dog, so use the heel of the hand over the widest portion of the rib cage, and use the heel of the second hand on top of the first hand to increase the pressure. Keep both elbows straight and push down firmly to squeeze the chest to one-quarter to one-third of its width.
- Compress for one count, then release for one count. Continue at the 80 rate per minute. With only one person present, administer a nose breath after every five chest compressions.
- Continue CPR for at least 10 minutes, hopefully until the dog breathes on his own and has a rhythmic pulse. If these signs do not appear after 10 minutes, recovery hopes are slender.

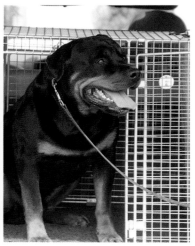

You must allow your dog sufficient ventilation when he is in a car, as temperatures can build up very rapidly.

RESCUE BREATHING

Provided the dog is not frightened or aggressive, mouth-to-nose respiration can be used in many circumstances and is unlikely ever to do harm. The air you breathe out of your lungs contains extra carbon dioxide, which, by itself, will stimulate a dog to breathe deeper.

- Lay the dog flat on his side. Pull the tongue out and hold it so it lies level with the front canine teeth, then close the mouth shut.
- Place your mouth over the dog's nose and blow gently into the nostrils. Look for the chest rising as it expands. Then release your mouth from the nose and let the air come out: excess air will come out through the lips, preventing any over distension of stomach or lungs.

- If the chest does not rise, next time blow more forcefully, holding the lips sealed with your hand.
- Continue at the rate of 20 to 30 breaths a minute, the lower rate for the larger type of dog. Keep this rate going until the dog breathes on his own or as long as the heart beats.

HEAT STROKE

Dogs most commonly suffer from heat exhaustion after they are left in a glass-roofed area or confined in a car without free access to drinking water. Dogs lose heat by panting air over their wet tongues. Once the moisture dries up, the dog suffers from heat exhaustion; there is no sweat mechanism, as in humans, to cool the body.

Death will ensue as the blood thickens and heart failure develops. The brachycephalic (short-nosed) breeds are at greatest risk. The predicted sequence of events in heat stroke are:

- The rectal temperature rises from 38.3 to 43.3 (104 to 110 F).
- With shock the lips turn grey. Panting is laboured.
- The dog may suffer with bloody diarrhoea.
- Coma and death can follow rapidly.

FIRST-AID MEASURES

- It is essential to get the dog out of the confined space as quickly as possible. If necessary, ask a police officer to break the car window if the

owner of the vehicle is missing!
- Lay the dog out flat, pour cold water over the whole body, or use a hosepipe to produce rapid cooling.
- Keep the mouth open and avoid water being breathed in.
- Apply CPR (as above) if necessary.
- Place the wet dog in front of an electric fan if available.
- When the rectal temperature is down to (103 F), stop the wetting and dry the dog; rubbing vigorously with a towel helps the circulation.
- Take the dog to the vet, where cold intravenous fluids can be given to thin and cool the blood in the circulation. A cold-water enema can also be used to prevent shock and other complications.

COLLAPSE

The term 'collapse' includes a variety of conditions that cause the dog to lay inert on the ground. If there is no obvious cause, then suspect some form of heart attack causing circulatory failure. Gundogs have been known to collapse while working, caused by a fall in the blood sugar level: the liver can only store so much glycogen from previous meals, and when this is used up after strenuous exercise for hours at a time, the sugar level drops and the dog can no longer work. A cereal bar with a sweet content is the best way of giving first-aid, as feeding the complex carbohydrate restores alertness. Non-working

NOSE BLEEDS

These are not as common in dogs as in humans, but they can be alarming if the dog has injured himself by colliding with a glass door or a brick wall. Spontaneous nose bleeds are seen in racing Greyhounds where the blood pressure has increased suddenly at the end of or during severe exercise.

FIRST-AID MEASURES

Cold ice packs can be difficult to apply, as the dog resents anything cold close to his eyes. It is possible to plug the nose with an astringent, such as tincture of achillea, which comes from the yarrow plant. Roll up cotton wool into a tight cone about the size of the dog's nostril opening. After moistening, you may be able to insert the cotton wool plug to stem the flow of blood. Make sure it can come out again, but your hand may cup the end of the nose long enough for the astringent to go inside, especially if the head is held up high. If the dog becomes distressed, do not persist, but move the dog to a place where the spray of blood will do least harm.

dogs that are allowed to exercise by slow walking can use their own fat reserves to provide sugar and are much less likely to collapse for this reason.

FIRST-AID FOR THE COLLAPSED PET DOG

- Move the dog cautiously for fear of making the situation worse. Generally, the best plan is to roll the dog into a blanket for transport home or to the vet. Again, ensure a clear airway and apply CPR if indicated by the signs.
- Call the vet. In heart disease, it is important to get the dog to the vet as quickly as possible. Collapse may be of short duration, if it is a cause similar to human fainting, but a

thorough veterinary examination after the event is advised.

HAEMORRHAGE

Bleeding is frightening to the onlooker, but the healthy dog has good natural blood-clotting mechanisms that, with a little assistance from the first-aider, will prevent shock and loss of life.

Don't wipe a wound that has stopped bleeding or is gently oozing, as this will dislodge the clot. Applying pressure over the bleeding area is the most effective and safe first-aid measure.

- Don't pour hydrogen peroxide or disinfectants on a fresh wound, as this can start a fresh

round of blood loss or kill healthy cells.

- Use sterile gauze pads or a pad of moistened cotton wool (or, for emergency use, the inside folded area of your handkerchief or a tissue) directly to the wound.
- Grip the area and apply direct pressure for 5 to 10 minutes. Don't peep under the pad.
- Next apply a bandage directly over it and get the dog to the vet surgery as soon as possible.
- Watch for signs of swelling of the leg below the pressure pad; generally speaking, a tight tourniquet is not recommended, as it will impair the normal circulation and cause pooling of blood and lymph fluids.

A dog may need to be prevented from exacerbating an injury by wearing an Elizabethan collar.

• If you have to apply a tourniquet (these can be improvised from a length of cloth, a tie, a belt or rope twisted with a stick) until the bleeding stops, the tight band must be released at least once every 10 minutes, three minutes would be considered safer. The tight band must be placed above the bleeding wound, on the side nearer to the heart to reduce the flow of arterial blood to the deep cut or injury.

• Next, call the vet.

• In all cases of severe bleeding, the aim is to get the dog to the vet as soon as possible. Internal bleeding, as if after a road collision, is difficult to recognise. Seek veterinary advice as soon as possible.

EYE INJURIES

Seeing an eyeball hanging out on a stalk after a dog fight is a frightening experience – and it is more than likely that the dog will lose the sight of that eye. It is more common to have tearing of the eyelids since dogs blink or close their eyes to protect them during a fight.

Call the vet. Eyelid wounds will need suturing in the surgery with anaesthesia, otherwise the face may heal uneven and scarred.

A corneal wound to the front of the eyeball can happen after a cat scratch or something penetrating the eye, such as a blackthorn. Haemorrhage into the eye may result and a blood-red swollen eye indicates the need for urgent veterinary attention.

FIRST-AID MEASURES

There are no real first-aid measures of value, but a pad of gauze moistened with normal (weak strength: 1 gram to 100 ml) salt solution can be placed over the eye if the dog will allow you to hold it there. Remember, eyes are sensitive and most injuries are painful. Aspirin could be used as an immediate anti-inflammatory – use small quarter-strength tablets for small dogs and once only. Try to prevent the dog rubbing at the eye by bandaging his forepaws or improvise an Elizabethan collar by using an inverted plastic bucket with its bottom cut out to fit the neck.

Call the vet whenever in doubt.

TIPS FOR GIVING MEDICINE

Chapter 5

Fortunately, vets like using injections in the surgery and this provides an almost immediate route for the medication to get to work. It is then necessary for the dog owner to give the pills or liquid medicines to maintain the benefit of the drug. Failure to give these medicines at home may lead to a part cure only or a condition that develops resistance to treatment. Recent studies by vets have shown that there is not infrequent 'non-compliance' where a course of medicine is not completed or sometimes not even started! This not unexpected, as human medication is similarly discarded by patients.

Older dogs with conditions such as arthritis or heart disease may require daily medication for the rest of their lives. It is fortunate that medicine manufacturers are aware of the difficulties of dosing and provide 'palatable' tablets and liquids. In the USA it is possible to have prescriptions made up with any one of five separate flavours, and you can choose the one with the flavour the dog likes best!

HOW TO DOSE THE DIFFICULT DOG

Most tablets are coated to disguise the contents.

- Take a small quantity of the dog's normal food and offer it to the dog.
- The next slightly larger portion should contain the tablet.
- After a further interval, offer the rest of the dog's daily ration so the dog remains hungry until the end of the meal.

If you adopt this procedure, the dog will not eat around the tablet and refuse any medication the next time. Only very few medicines need to be given when the stomach is empty.

Another aid in dosing is to talk your dog into cooperation! Speak to the dog, asking him to open his mouth, and, with persistence, this may happen (use reward training by voice praise). Then place the medication to the back of the tongue of the open mouth. Always offer praise and, after giving medication, follow it with a reward, such as cheese or sausage meat.

Other techniques are to fold the tablet into a paste-consistency food when the dog is hungry after smelling other food being prepared. Bread and butter or soft cheese can be used as a 'treat with a tablet'. Cheese is another favourite way of disguising a tablet, especially if the dog is used to morsels of cheese provided during reward training.

Many ill dogs requiring medication have little or no

GIVING MEDICATION

The tablet should be placed on the back of the tongue.

It may be easier to give liquid medicine with a syringe.

appetite and the above methods may be without avail. In this case, try the following:

- Open the dog's mouth and get the tablet to the very back of the tongue. To induce the dog to swallow, hold the face upwards.
- If the dog is likely to struggle, you may need an assistant to steady or cradle the dog in their arm. This allows you to use both hands to part the lips near the space between the canine and molar teeth. If you insert the thumb into this toothless gap and press upwards on the roof of the dog's mouth, the dog will then invariably open his mouth.
- The dog will keep his mouth open as long as you continue to press on the hard palate. The free hand can then be used to lob the tablet to the very back of the tongue.
- Then release the thumb pressure, hold the mouth shut

with the nose tilted in the air until the dog is seen to swallow. Try to make this more pleasurable by then offering a small treat.

- You can also try moistening the lips with water to assist swallowing as the tablet reaches the very back of the throat.
- A water-filled syringe could also be used to wash the mouth and to stop the dog holding on to the tablet at the back of his dry mouth.

Another aid is to use soft, palatable dough that is moulded around the tablet given to the dog. 'Pillease' can be obtained from veterinary surgeons, and its stickiness and its palatability means the dog cannot lick off the required medication.

LIQUID MEDICINES
Liquid medicines can more easily be incorporated in the dog's

food, making it easier for your dog to accept. If the dog will not eat his food, you will need to give medicine from a spoon – metal or plastic. When trying to give medicine off a teaspoon:

- Approach the side of the mouth, pull up the lower lip and pour into the gap between the canine and molar teeth as described above.
- Keep the head up high until gulping movements show the medicine is going down.
- Some people will stroke the throat under the chin to assist swallowing.
- A plastic syringe from the vet may be easier to use than a teaspoon when giving liquids.

If you have to work on your own, get the dog into a quiet corner to prevent him backing away from you; alternatively, take the dog between your knees and give the tablet from behind the dog's head.

PART II

COMMON DISEASE PROBLEMS

DISEASES AND DISORDERS OF THE SENSORY ORGANS

The organs of special senses include the eyes, the ears, the nose, the tongue (for taste) and those for balance. The ear contains receptors that are adapted to respond to sound waves and in the bony part to balance. It is in this way that infections of the outer ear may lead to loss of balance if the semi-circular canals of the inner ear are damaged. Each organ is interlinked through nerve paths through the brain, so the dog with inner ear disease, as well as dizziness and loss of balance, may show rapid jerking movements of the eyeballs known as nystagmus.

EYES

CLOUDING, BULGING OF THE EYES, SQUINTING

Any one of these signs suggests a severe eye problem needing urgent veterinary care. Watery eyes and squints are signs of a very painful eye and anaesthetic eye drops may be required.

Causes: The causes of these three eye conditions could be:

- Infection of the eye with damage to the cornea (the transparent window of the eye) known as keratitis. Inflammation damages the cornea and a painful ulcer can develop. In the longstanding

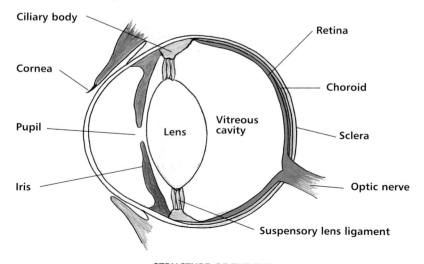

Ciliary body

Cornea

Pupil

Iris

Lens

Vitreous cavity

Retina

Choroid

Sclera

Optic nerve

Suspensory lens ligament

STRUCTURE OF THE EYE

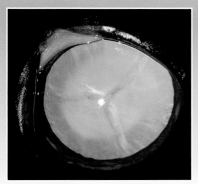

Cataract in the lens of the eye.

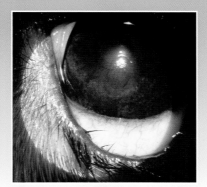

Distichiasis: Caused by abnormal lashes at the edge of eyelid.

Ectropion: The condition is caused by drooping lower eyelids.

problem, scarring and black pigment is laid down, causing diminished vision. Some corneal diseases are inherited, such as the dry eye condition kerato-conjunctivitis sicca (KCS) most commonly found in the West Highland White Terrier.

- Increased pressure within the eye, known as glaucoma. If untreated, it can lead to complete loss of sight. A rise of fluid pressure is intensely painful, so treatment by the vet is urgent. In the more chronic form found in older dogs, sight is gradually lost due to pressure of fluid on the optic nerve.
- A cataract is an opacity of the lens of the eye; larger cataracts will have a permanent effect on vision. Some breeds of dog have inherited cataract or it may result from an injury to the eye.
- Irritation from dirt or specks of vegetable matter adhering to the eye surface.
- A thorn penetrating the cornea.
- The eyelashes can cause

problems: extra inward-turning ones (ectopic cilia), in-turning eyelashes (entropion), or abnormal lashes at the edge of the eyelid (distichiasis) are some other possibilities.

- Ectropion is caused by the lower lid drooping down and away. This can be an inherited fault.
- The third eyelid may become involved in any conjunctivitis where the cornea is inflamed. A bulging of the third eyelid is not uncommon in some hound breeds where it is known as 'cherry eye'.

Signs: The signs of eye problems are fairly obvious, although in the older dog the cloudy blueness of the eye will not always be recognised at first – the dog may stumble into objects in the half light in a room. Older dogs have synchesis scintillans due to minute particles developing in the chamber at the back of the eye, causing a bluish reflection, but it is often confused with

cataract as a lens opacity.

Treatment: Veterinary inspection using an ophthalmoscope (a light source with magnification is advised). Simple water-based ophthalmic eye drop (also used in humans) can be applied as a temporary measure. Antibiotic in the form of ointment or drops may be supplied by the vet. It is essential to stop a dog rubbing an itching eye since this can lead to corneal ulceration and, if the ulcer then goes deeper into the cornea, the whole eyeball may burst.

DISCHARGES FROM THE EYES, REDNESS AND WATERY EYES

A red eye is not uncommon in many breeds of dogs. Irritation of the lids with sticky or dry crusted eyelids, or a watery eye from the overflow of tears may be seen.

Causes: Conjunctivitis may be caused by bacterial or viral infections, pollens from walking through flowering grasses, from

Cherry eye: A bulging of the third eyelid.

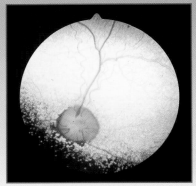

Retina showing progressive retinal atrophy.

in-growing eyelashes etc. The production of normal tears may be affected, causing a dry eye.

The tear film covers the eye to protect it and consists of three layers produced by the eye glands:
- An outer oily layer
- A watery moistening layer
- An inner slimy mucus layer

If tear production is altered after injury or certain chemical damage, a dry eye results with constant irritation. Itchy eyes mean the dog may scratch the eye surface, especially if there are dew claws on the feet.

Treatment: Try bandaging the fore paws, apply simple eye drops, then seek professional medication or other measures (such as the removal of foreign bodies). Removal of foreign matter will be necessary when a grass or oat seed lies on the surface or even when a thorn has stabbed into the cornea.

For those wishing to try a simple herbal remedy, the diluted tincture of Eyebright (*Euphrasia officinalis*) may be effective. Use two to three drops of this tincture in a cup of recently boiled water that is allowed to cool just below blood heat. Apply twice a day. There would be no alcohol left in the tincture since it would evaporate with the hot water. Twenty drops of the 1-3 tincture placed in 10 ml of water is a more accurate way of measuring the eye lotion.

FAILING EYESIGHT

Dogs use their sense of smell as much as their eyes to find their way and recognise places, so failing eyesight or blindness is not the worst handicap for a dog.

Causes: Any disorder that blocks the light getting to the nerve layers of the retina at the back of the eye can lead to impaired vision. Corneal disease, cataracts, and glaucoma are such examples, as well as degeneration of the eye nerves known as progressive retinal atrophy (PRA).

The retina, the light-sensitive area at the back of the eye, can be subject to inherited diseases that may lead to blindness. In collie breeds, the commonest disease is known as collie eye anomaly (CEA). It is recommended that all litters of pups from collie breeds should be examined for the signs of CEA. The severity of the condition varies from no real effect on sight to blindness following a detachment of the retina or bleeding inside the eye.

Progressive retinal atrophy (PRA) has become less common as a result of control schemes (in the UK operated by the Kennel Club and the British Veterinary

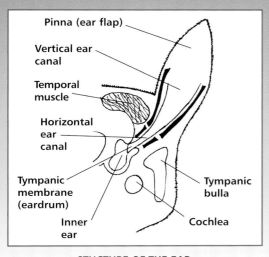

Pinna (ear flap)

Vertical ear canal

Temporal muscle

Horizontal ear canal

Tympanic membrane (eardrum)

Tympanic bulla

Inner ear

Cochlea

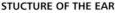

STUCTURE OF THE EAR

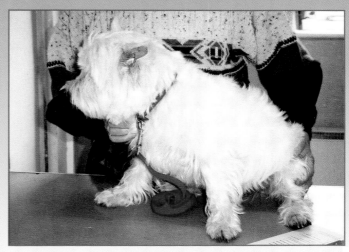

A West Highland White Terrier with its ear stitched after haematoma drainage.

Association in cooperation with breeders). Dogs affected with PRA have difficulty in seeing in dim light and they then gradually lose their ability to see in bright light, with eventual blindness.

Retinal dysplasia is another congenital disease, which can lead to a detached retina with sudden blindness.

Cataracts cause loss of vision; they may be hereditary but may be a sign of diabetes mellitus due to excess sugar collecting inside the lens.

Signs: Recognising blindness should not be difficult. However, the simple test of shining a torch at the eye and watching for the pupils to constrict is not always reliable. This is because the dog's retina or the visual part of the brain may not be able to form an image – rather like a camera with no film inserted. The response to

the dog walking in a dark room with rearranged furniture could be a better test.

Treatment: Treatment after diagnosis is best left to the vet. Some dietary supplements may assist in delaying degeneration of the retina and there are now very effective treatments for cataract and for glaucoma. Removal of the lens or dissolving it can be very effective in restoring vision so the dog can recognise objects and people, but they are unable to focus closely.

EARS

AURAL HAEMATOMA
Scratching at the ears may cause bleeding under the skin (aural haematoma). Painful if not treated, this will cause the ear flap to scar and crinkle. If treated surgically, the haematoma is drained and

usually the flap is then stitched to the cartilage. Post-operatively, an Elizabethan collar or a figure-of-eight head banadage may be applied.

DISCHARGES
Many dogs have greasy ears but the very smelly yellow type of ear discharge can hardly be missed.

Causes: The cause may be a bacterial infection, ear mites, or fungal and yeast infections. A foreign object may also be responsible.

Signs: Look for the dog that is constantly scratching at his ears or rubbing his head along the carpets. A grass seed in the ear can produce sudden pain and strange behaviour.

Treatment: It is important to have a veterinary inspection of

PART II

the deeper structures of the ear as soon as you suspect an ear problem in order to prevent the condition deteriorating. An ear swab may be taken, and, in most cases, you will be advised to follow a simple routine to clean and dry the canals. Follow-up home treatment can involve the application of drops or creams once or twice a day. A herbal approach for ear infection is to use an extract of green cleavers (*Galium aparine*), as it helps to remove fluids and is said to reduce itches internally.

HEARING WITH DIFFICULTY, DEAFNESS

Some degree of deafness is almost inevitable in the ageing dog. Deafness in puppies can be surprisingly difficult to recognise, as many signs may be put down to stubborn behaviour. There are special diagnostic centres for deafness that use the BAER test. It is a non-invasive test that records electrical activity to a series of clicks that can then be analysed by computers.

Causes: There is a strong hereditary link – 1 in 3,000 puppies are born deaf. This affects 50 or more breeds and includes the Dalmatian. Dogs with blue eyes are more likely to be deaf.

There are two types of deafness: those due to disorders of the hairs in the innermost (cochlear) organ (known as sensi-neural defects) and those due to

Deafness has a strong hereditary link, and the Dalmatian is one of the breeds most affected.

a conducting of sounds failure: from the ear drum across the middle ear. Deafness may be present from birth, as in the first form, or develop later with ageing or from disease – usually a chronic ear infection. As the brain ages, sensi-neural deafness may be one of the first signs, but it is unlikely to develop to a total loss of hearing.

Treatment: Ear drops to soften the ear drum may be tried. There is no specific treatment to alleviate deafness – it is more a matter of helping the dog to cope with the disability.

Older dogs that develop hearing loss are not such a problem as puppies, since the older dog knows the routines of the daily round. High-pitch whistles may be used or a companion dog may help the deaf dog to respond to audible 'cues'. Exaggerated hand signals and smell stimulants will also help a deaf dog to respond.

NOSE

PAWING AT THE NOSE, SNEEZING

The nose is a very important place for sensory nerve endings - remarkable feats of drug or explosive detection rely on minute quantities of olfactory stimulant agents. Other dogs are being trained for human cancer detection.

The external nostrils of the healthy dog may be slightly moist and the dog licks his nose to keep it that way. However, there should certainly be no excessive discharge from the nostrils. Sneezing is an important sign of nasal irritation.

Causes:
- Allergies – sneezing with a watery discharge and rubbing at the face is an important sign of canine atopy (see p. 123 in skin section)
- A grass seed or barley awn up the nose – these may prove difficult to remove and cause persisting sneezing and a pus-like nasal discharge
- Viral rhinitis is associated with

A grass seed in the nose can cause sneezing or nasal discharge.

Scaly nose on a Boxer caused by furunculosis skin disease.

PART II

kennel cough (see pp. 86-87) but it may cause a watery nose with sneezing but no cough

• Nasal aspergillosis as a fungal infection in dogs can cause a thick nasal discharge and even nose bleeds

Treatment: For all these conditions the vet may prescribe a sedative antihistamine or make an internal examination with an endoscope to see up the nose.

NASAL FURUNCULOSIS

Furunculosis is a deep skin infection often associated with some underlying disease (such as an underactive thyroid, Demodex or fungal infection). When scaly pustules, crusts and hair loss appear on the muzzle, it is particularly unsightly, but furunculosis may also be found on the flanks, anal region or elsewhere on the body. It is often necessary to find the underlying cause before long-term antibiotic medication is used, often in conjunction with mild antiseptic washes. In severe cases, surgical drainage of deep cavities may be required under anaesthesia.

NASAL SOLAR DERMATITIS

This is mainly found in collie breeds but can become more common due to higher risks of exposure to ultra violet light. Crusts and ulceration of the skin of the nose develop with the dog pawing at his itchy face.

The use of plastic dog bowls can sometimes cause irritation, with a loss of nose pigment, crusting of the lips and the nose. The use of stainless steel or ceramic dog bowls would remove a possible aggravating cause if the dog has become sensitised to dyestuffs as well.

Treatment: The use of a waterproof sunblock applied over the nose can be effective, as long as the dog does not lick it off. Applied sparingly, just before the dog goes out for a walk, he will be more distracted from licking and less likely to remove the cream. Your vet may be able to recommend other treatments where appropriate.

THE MOUTH AND TEETH

Chapter 7

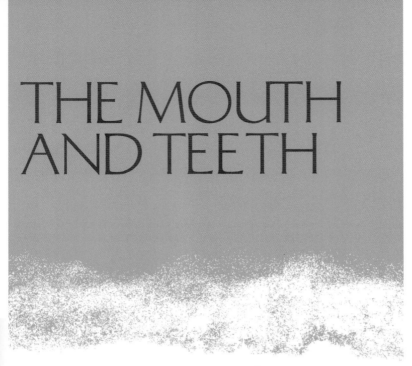

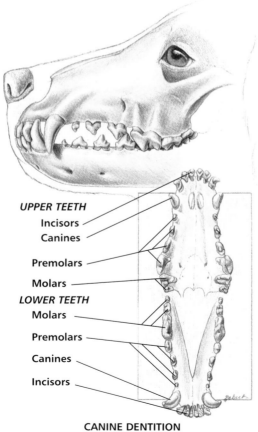

UPPER TEETH
Incisors
Canines
Premolars
Molars
LOWER TEETH
Molars
Premolars
Canines
Incisors

CANINE DENTITION

Hill's Atlas of Veterinary Clinical Anatomy

The mouth is surrounded by the lips, which help to keep the food and saliva in place before the dog swallows his food. There are four pairs of salivary glands that are important in digestion. Saliva is alkaline, and contains some enzymes and antibacterial substances that help to reduce dangerous bacteria gaining entry to the digestive tract.

BREATH & OFFENSIVE ODOURS
Bad breath is not only unpleasant for the owner – it can indicate a number of painful mouth conditions.

Causes: A most unpleasant smell will come from an abscess of the tooth root. The mouth is very painful and pus can be seen oozing from around a tooth, causing a foul smell. If your face

Warts may be seen as small growths at the lip edges.

A Bichon Frisé with a cyst in its mouth.

is anywhere near such a dog, you will have to recoil. However, the worst smell comes from dogs with lip fold pyoderma (see pp. 85 and 124). The putrefying smell is commonest in the spaniel breeds with lip folds and grooves that saliva trickles into. Food remains in these places, leading to an infection of the soggy lip folds.

There are other less common reasons for persisting bad breath:

- A foreign body wedged in the mouth, such as a stick or cane across the roof of the mouth or a chewed bone fragment stuck between the teeth
- Plant awns can burrow under the tongue
- String from an elastic meat wrapper stuck around the tongue should always be searched for by opening the mouth in a bright light
- Tumours, such as warts, can be found in the mouth. A common tumour in Boxers is known as epulis, and it has been seen in other breeds of dogs. Epulis consist of a fleshy flap of hard gum that may grow so big as to be chewed between the teeth
- Periodontal disease and other dental problems are quite common in the gums below or under the teeth.

Treatment: Treatment means removing the cause and treating any infections with an appropriate antibiotic. Dental hygiene is important. As a preventative measure, consider regular tooth brushing and lip wiping after meals. Treatment of epulis will usually involve a surgical operation under general anaesthesia to remove the fleshy growths.

CHOMPING & CHEWING

Puppies change from milk teeth to the permanent teeth between three and seven months of age. The shedding of the milk teeth makes puppies want to chew more. A behaviour problem may develop with mouthing at the offered hand or, more likely, chewing furniture, rugs and other undesirable activities.

Causes:

- Any foreign body stuck in the mouth will cause a sudden onset of chewing and salivation. A hard toffee or a piece of bone may get stuck on a back tooth.
- The Boxer with an epulis will be constantly chewing and flecks of blood appear in the saliva.
- Painful warty growths caused by a papilloma virus may appear; benign tumours may be seen as small warts at the lip edges – up to 50 may be present. They start as tiny white lumps on the gum and then may grow broccoli-shaped masses up to 1 cm. They are usually self-limiting as the body overcomes the virus; they can disappear after a few weeks or months. They usually occur in dogs under two years of age.
- A previously normal dog found subdued with a wet front and saliva all round his muzzle may have consumed an irritant or a poison.
- A dog that has an epileptic fit will chew frantically, salivate

excessively and may show other signs of struggling. If you were not present at the time or never knew the dog to be subject to epilepsy, the wrong conclusion might be drawn. Some fits never get worse than the chewing stage.

Treatment: A detailed examination is necessary before the cause and the correction of the chewing can be provided. Puppies can be given soft objects to mouth on if they are teething. Some adult dogs have a tendency to chew – usually as a result of boredom. In this instance you can provide hard chews or 'boredom buster' toys that keep the dog occupied for some time while trying to get at a store of food concealed in the toy.

DRIBBLING & DROOLING

A certain amount of drooling can be expected in breeds with loose, hanging-down lips. Saliva is produced in the mouth in response to the stimuli of food smells and the anticipation of a meal. The saliva contains mucus to lubricate the food as it is swallowed; there are also some weak digestive enzymes but saliva is 99 per cent water. Saliva has the important function of cooling the body through the tongue as the dog pants.

Causes: There are a number of reasons why a dog may produce an abnormal quantity of saliva:
• Poisonous substances, such as

Gum disease, plus a heavy build-up of tartar on the teeth.

organophosphates, which are toxic chemical substances found in some herbicides and pesticides
• Pain
• Fear
• As a precursor to vomiting
• Cracking of the lips, known as cheilitis, should be looked for; crusts may be seen
• Mouth burns
• Lacerations of the tongue or mouth after a dog has licked a tin can or a sharp object
• Stomatitis – an inflammation inside the mouth
• Periodontal disease and gingivitis

GUMS AND TONGUE DISORDERS

The appearance of the gums gives an indication of the state of the circulation or anaemia (see p. 83). In order to check for any changes, you need to raise the lips near the canine tooth. To inspect the whole mouth, insert the thumb and press upwards on the hard palate. This method is also used

to open the mouth for giving tablets (see p. 42). For signs of a healthy mouth, see p. 12.

Causes:
• The edges of the gums should fit tightly around each tooth. When there is gingivitis (inflammation of the gums) chalky calculus builds up at the tooth base. This pushes back the gum margin, allowing pocketing rather than the preferred tight seal. The pockets trap old food, and saliva encourages mouth bacteria to multiply, leading to bad breath. The gums appear red and swollen; they may bleed if rubbed or pus can be expressed from the gum margin.
• Periodontitis develops as the next stage of dental disease. Teeth become loose and could drop out or, for molar teeth, result in a root abscess. This is often not seen until a painful swelling develops below the eye, which may burst and ooze pus on to the face.
• A blue tinge to the gums as well as the tongue and lips could indicate poor oxygen supply, as found with heart diseases (see p. 81), lung tumours (see p. 80) or pneumonia (see p. 79).
• A fluid-filled cyst just beneath the tongue might be seen, known as a ranula. It consists of retained saliva from the sublingual salivary glands. The condition usually resolves without the need for surgical interference.

PART II

• Paralysis of the tongue (fortunately now quite rare) was caused by nerve damage after distemper virus infection, leaving the dog's tongue hanging down out of the mouth and quite dry. This is occasionally seen in older dogs that have had a 'stroke'. Lapping is impossible and the dog needs a deep bowl to suck up the water in the way a horse drinks.

Treatment: In the case of gum disease, treatment is by professional tooth cleaning. A change of diet to a firmer or more fibrous food may help. Aftercare at home could involve tooth brushing (see below).

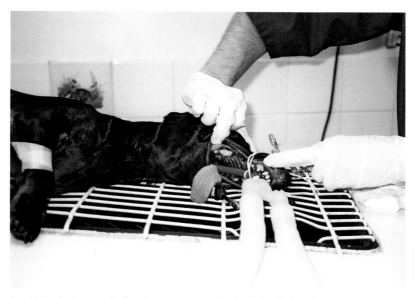

Dentistry being carried out on an anaesthetised Dachshund.

TOOTH DECAY & DENTAL PROBLEMS

Once a dog has changed his milk teeth, usually at around six months, the next set have to last the rest of the dog's life. It is not unusual to find a temporary canine remaining just behind the new canine tooth. This can cause some of the problems described above and it is necessary to extract the temporaries if they have not gone by nine months old. Most breeds then have 42 adult teeth in the mouth.

Causes: Tooth decay occurs after a dog breaks the protective crown from the tooth, exposing the sensitive pulp cavity. Periodontitis is common in the older dog. The gum infection attacks the cement and the attaching tooth membrane, and, as the root

becomes infected, the teeth loosen and may drop out.

Sometimes tooth cavities are seen in the molars of dogs, appearing as a black spot or food-filled, if on the tooth crown. Cavities will become painful and lead to a tooth abscess.

Treatment: Specialist veterinary dentistry has encouraged root canal therapy and can save teeth. Abscessed roots, broken teeth and malocclusions (where the teeth do not meet each other) may also benefit from specialist dental treatment, but costs are a consideration with anything more than simple extractions.

BRUSHING THE TEETH AND GUMS

By the time the dog is two or three years, a programme of

dental care may be needed, involving scaling and polishing.

It is a fact that eight out of 10 dogs over the age of three years have some degree of dental disease. The best plan is to adopt a regime of teeth cleaning from the very start.

• A young puppy at first will think it is a game and the toothbrush will be chewed up if left about.

• If the puppy is too wriggly, use some special meat-flavour toothpaste for dogs, rubbing it on his gums once a day to get him used to the flavour and sensation of having his gums touched.

• At six months the tooth brushing can become part of the day's grooming routine. It will help to avoid costly dental bills later in life. Many dogs do

PART II

not require veterinary dental care and prevention in the home saves costly bills.

- There are several good dog toothpastes and dental products to use: a rubber thimble is an alternative to the long-handled toothbrush. The gums, as well as the teeth, should be brushed, at a 45-degree angle, using the finger brush or the toothbrush.
- Lift the lips to expose the outer surfaces of the teeth in the mouth. Rub the teeth and gums in a circular motion to massage them – as this will help prevent receding gums. It is difficult to do the inner surface, but the tongue keeps this side in

Regular brushing will keep the teeth clean and healthy.

better shape usually.
- The most important part to brush is along the border of the tooth and gum, to delay or avoid periodontitis.

Clean the teeth on a regular basis at least once a week or daily if you can give the time. It is important not to use human toothpaste, as these are not formulated to be swallowed.

Note: Dental chews or leathery toys can help the dog in cleaning his own teeth. A hard baked marrowbone can be offered but should only be given when the dog is under supervision. Anticipate that two dogs will squabble if only one bone is provided.

DIGESTIVE PROBLEMS

The digestive system is the important route whereby food is taken in, swallowed, and broken down to release all the necessary nutrients; the waste is disposed of, together with some other excreted products, in the faeces. Dogs can digest a highly varied diet and take in nutrients from digested food by a process of absorption.

The digestive system can be divided into seven areas

- Mouth and teeth
- Oesophagus (or gullet)
- Stomach
- Small intestine
- Large intestine
- Rectum and anus
- The liver, pancreas and other glands that aid digestion.

ABDOMINAL PAIN AND TENDERNESS

Only close observation of the dog's normal behaviour will suggest if pain is present. There may be a tense expression of the face and ears (ears pinned back), and a reluctance to move, with the dog often lying on the coldest surface possible (suggesting abdominal pain). Some dogs will whine or cry, but most will try to lie as still as possible; other dogs may pace around, not being able to settle. These signs may be first noticed if a dog refuses to eat and a digestive system disorder is developing.

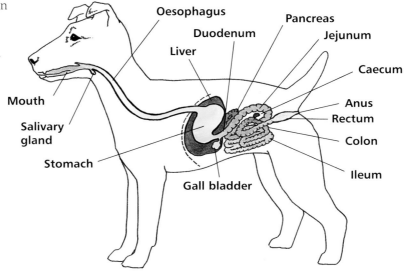

THE DIGESTIVE SYSTEM

Causes: As well as the more obvious digestive problems and infections, one should consider other possible causes of abdominal pain.

- Gas distension – see Bloat (see p. 59)
- Gastro enteritis – inflammation of the stomach and intestines (see p. 60)
- Hepatitis – inflammation of the liver (see p. 62)
- Peritonitis – inflammation of the lining of the abdominal cavity
- Internal injury (from road accident or being kicked) – a ruptured spleen, crushed kidney or ruptured bladder may have resulted
- Urinary stones, known as calculi, can cause pain when they obstruct
- Poisoning
- Cancers – some, like gastric tumours, may be very aggressive; others cause pressure with partial obstructions
- Acute pancreatitis – see below.

There are many other causes of abdomen pain: gas distending the intestines (see below); Campylobacters cause a gassy enteritis; or intussusception (inward-turning of the bowel tube – see p. 58) in puppies and peritonitis. Uraemia, either due to kidney disease or urinary tract obstruction, causes repeated

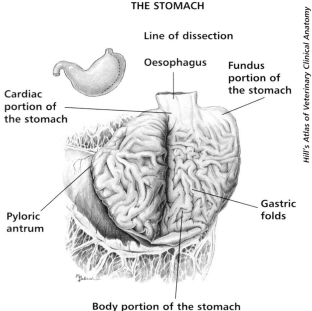

THE STOMACH

Line of dissection

Oesophagus

Fundus portion of the stomach

Cardiac portion of the stomach

Gastric folds

Pyloric antrum

Body portion of the stomach

Hill's Atlas of Veterinary Clinical Anatomy

vomiting. It is necessary for tests to be performed before appropriate treatment is given.

Treatment: If pain is longer than a short duration, the attendance at a veterinary clinic is advised so tests can be performed and appropriate measures taken. There are specific drugs that act on the intestinal tract and can relieve pain.

ACUTE PANCREATITIS
The pancreas is an internal organ that produces digestive juices. If the pancreas becomes inflamed, often for no obvious reason, symptoms can develop suddenly into a severe illness, with collapse followed by shock and death.

Treatment: The treatment of acute pancreatitis requires

immediate hospitalisation, with intensive care treatment for shock combined with intravenous fluids and pain relief.

Some recent authorities suggest fluids given by mouth for the first few days, together with sieved baby rice, may help aid recovery. Bovril meat extract as a low-fat flavouring can be added later to make the rice more interesting. Antibiotics, pain killers and a low-fat diet will be prescribed to continue treatment.

Acute flare-ups require the same treatment as dogs with chronic pancreatitis and there is the same risk of a fatal outcome.

DIARRHOEA & DYSENTERY
Loose faeces contain more water than ideal and in diarrhoea the slime (from extra mucus), undigested food and water create a large volume and frequent bowel emptying movements. Dysentery describes the situation when blood is also seen in the loose faeces.

Causes: There are many causes of diarrhoea. It can be the way of the body removing unsuitable food obtained after scavenging or eating an over-fatty meal. Dogs can experience diarrhoea when they are excited or upset. The rapid transit of partially digested food in the stomach will mean that the

PART II

THE SMALL INTESTINE

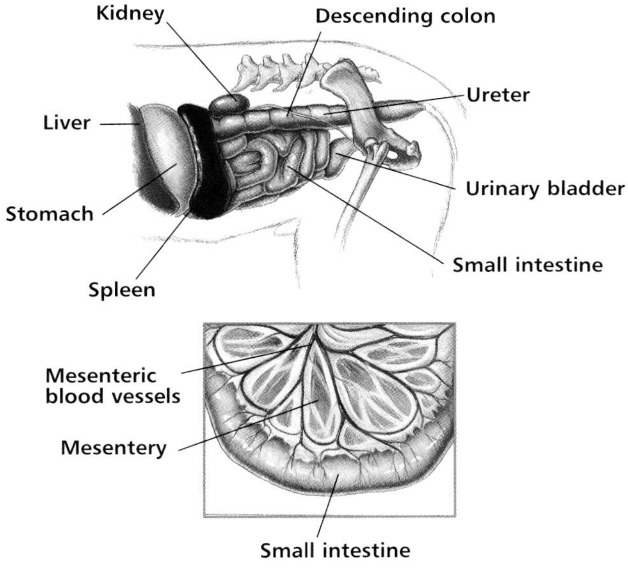

Kidney
Descending colon
Ureter
Liver
Urinary bladder
Stomach
Small intestine
Spleen

Mesenteric blood vessels
Mesentery
Small intestine

THE COLON

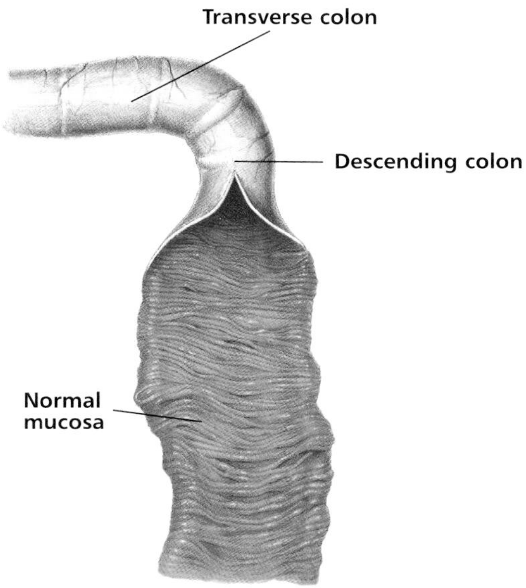

Transverse colon
Descending colon
Normal mucosa

Hill's Atlas of Veterinary Clinical Anatomy

PART II

usual 80 per cent reabsorption of water in the intestine fails to happen and liquid faeces squirt out with unpleasant odour. Any sudden change of diet may cause diarrhoea.

There are many causes of persisting diarrhoea:
- Parasites – worms, Giardia
- Food intolerance or hypersensitivity (see p. 58)
- Canine inflammatory bowel disease, colitis (see p. 58)
- Bacteria such as Campylobacter, E. coli, Salmonellae
- Viral – parvovirus was a new disease in the late 1970s, causing a high fatality in puppies. This virus and other viruses still occur from time to time
- Foreign bodies
- Growths and cancer

- Maldigestion (exocrine pancreatic insufficiency EPI, see p. 61)

Treatment: In the first instance it is necessary to decide what type of diarrhoea is present. Persisting diarrhoea (more than 48 hours) needs veterinary investigation and a number of tests may be required to effect a cure. Sudden acute diarrhoea attacks are best treated by starvation for 24 hours but allow the dog to drink as much as it needs providing this does not cause vomiting.

Seek veterinary treatment if the diarrhoea is accompanied by repeated vomiting or if the faeces are black and tarry or have a quantity of blood. Balanced salt solutions (often known as electrolyte replacement) and/or some anti-diarrhoea compound

to slow intestine motility (known as anti-spasmodics) may be kept on hand for the dog that persistently scavenges.

On return to offering food, use a low-fat, bland diet; traditionally boiled rice and skinless chicken are used. Dairy products and milk are probably best avoided, as some dogs cannot digest these due to lactase deficiency. However, it is usually safe to offer soft cottage cheese together with the cooked rice or a plain pasta. Other possibilities include mashed cooked potato and white fish. These should be fed for several days before gradually returning to normal food.

CANINE INFLAMMATORY BOWEL DISEASE
Often recognised as any inflammation in the

gastrointestinal tract, where no cause can be recognised (idiopathic). Crohns disease and ulcerative colitis in humans have their equivalent in dogs where they are called lymphocytic-plasmacytic, eosinophilic, granulomatous IBD. Colitis is a similar condition that affects individual dogs; causes may include an immune response to antigens in the colon when it is known as eosinophilic colitis.

Treatment: Long-term treatment may be necessary with diet adjustments. Prednisolone (a steroid) and sulphasalazine are the drugs most commonly used. Antibiotics such as metronidazole, tylosin oxytetracycline are also used to reduce bowel bacteria. Combinations of two or more of these may be tried and the immunosuppressive drug azathioprine can be used when other treatments have not been successful. Supplements with probiotics help to restore normal healthy bacteria in the intestines.

The herbal medicine practitioner may advise extracts of wild chamomile (*Matricaria*

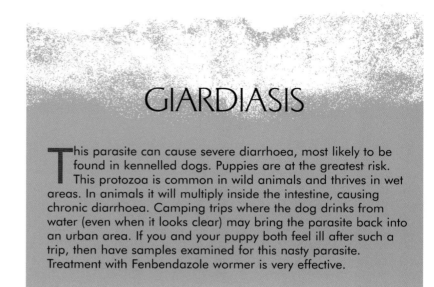

GIARDIASIS

This parasite can cause severe diarrhoea, most likely to be found in kennelled dogs. Puppies are at the greatest risk. This protozoa is common in wild animals and thrives in wet areas. In animals it will multiply inside the intestine, causing chronic diarrhoea. Camping trips where the dog drinks from water (even when it looks clear) may bring the parasite back into an urban area. If you and your puppy both feel ill after such a trip, then have samples examined for this nasty parasite. Treatment with Fenbendazole wormer is very effective.

recutita) for colitis and inflammatory bowel disease, and it is considered safe for young animals, too.

FOOD INTOLERANCES
These may manifest as chronic skin disease, associated with itchy, red or watery eyes and repeated diarrhoea attacks. Food intolerance has also been associated with some behaviour problems.

Protein foods are chiefly to blame: beef, pork, chicken, eggs,

fish, dairy products, spices, wheat, maize, and soya bean have all been incriminated and, of course, many commercial foods contain one or more of these products. An elimination diet may be tried, especially for those food allergies causing skin disease. A novel diet (such as cooked rabbit and boiled swede) may be one such mixture fed, exclusive to any other food (including treats) for six weeks, to see if the symptoms go away. Suspected foods can then be added one by one to the exclusion diet until an adverse response is seen. An improvement, followed by deterioration on returning to the former diet, is characteristic. Once identification is obtained, it may be possible to find a special commercial diet made up without the trigger food; alternatively, a home-prepared diet with occasional oil, mineral

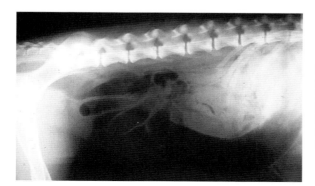

X-ray of the abdomen showing intussusception (inward turning of the bowel tube) seen as intestinal obstruction.

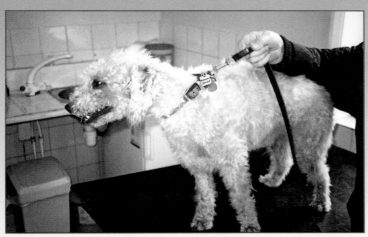

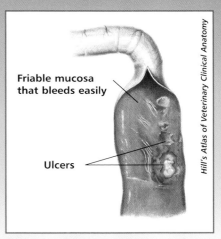

A Bedlington Terrier suffering from chronic colitis.

CHRONIC COLITIS

Friable mucosa
that bleeds easily

Ulcers

Hill's Atlas of Veterinary Clinical Anatomy

and vitamin supplements will help the dog.

Another approach is based on the idea of the 'leaky gut', one that is too permeable to large molecules that can be absorbed as the food is consumed. These partly digested food particles go straight into the blood stream from the vessel supplying the intestines. Herbalists use tinctures of calendula with other similar herbal products for 'leaky gut syndrome' and this is said to reduce food intolerance.

BLOATED OR DISTENDED ABDOMEN

The stomach lies on the left side but the whole of the abdomen may seem distended, bulging behind the rib cage. Distension may be seen soon after feeding or be present all the time.

Causes: As well as stomach gas known as gastric tympany, causing the abdomen distension, other causes should be considered:

- Ascites – fluid in the abdomen, commonly called 'dropsy' in former times. It can occur in chronic heart disease.
- Cushing's disease – an endocrine disease of older dogs where the adrenal gland produces excess hormone. There is a weakening of the muscles, giving the characteristic 'pot-bellied' appearance. The dog is short of energy, often with loss of hair over the body.
- Gastric dilatation volvulus (GDV). Bloat or gastric tympany is a life-threatening condition recognised by a gas-filled stomach bulging out more on the left side, where a drum-like resonance can be found on tapping the skin. It is caused by gas accumulation; a twist in the stomach entrance

(volvulus) may prevent release by belching. Death will result after an hour or so from shock, with pressure on the heart and lungs and restriction of the blood flow.

It is believed that tympany is not the result of food fermenting in the stomach but due to the dog swallowing air as he eats. Dogs affected are deep chested, often older, and the condition may be related to a nervous temperament. It was common in large breeds of gundogs, often fed at the end of the day when tired; dogs trained in kennels are now fed first thing in the working day and the death rate from gastric tympany is non-existent.

Treatment: The dog must be taken to the surgery or vet hospital as quickly as possible. The dog will be put on to fluid therapy for shock and then the

A terrier with a swollen abdomen caused by ascites.

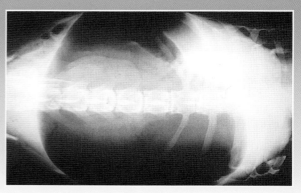

X-ray showing gastric dilatation.

slow release of the gas will be needed. This may be possible using a fine stomach tube to negotiate a twist at the entrance to the stomach (torsion nearly always develops with the bloat) or a large bore needle or trochar will be inserted into the left side of the distended abdomen. It is best not to be in the desperate situation where you have to pierce the stomach yourself to stop death by asphyxiation. Surgical procedures involve decompression of the stomach gas, untwisting and possibly fixing the stomach in a way so that it cannot rotate another time if dilatation reoccurs.

SICKNESS, VOMITING, REGURGITATION OF FOOD

The dog is known as a vomiting species and can get rid of any stomach overload or toxic food by returning it outside without any great effort. Regurgitation means that the food has only just gone down into the oesophagus, barely reaching the stomach

before it is returned so it will still look like food. Vomiting is the forceful expulsion of the stomach contents, which will smell sour and is often stained yellowish from bile.

There are two likely causes of regurgitation:

- An obstruction in the oesophagus. A knob of gristle, a chop bone, or a small toy is the most likely cause of regurgitation and needs emergency treatment to dislodge or remove the blockage. Partial obstructions are most common in terrier breeds where it may be possible for the dog to take in liquids still.
- Chronic regurgitation, accompanied by drooling, may be due to injury to the entrance to the stomach, a stricture (narrowing), or a weak, flabby-muscled oesophagus, known as megaoesophagus. Seen as an acquired condition of older dogs, it may also be

congenital, developing once a puppy is weaned off milky foods.

Treatment: Simple vomiting is best treated by resting the stomach. This means stopping food for 12-24 hours, permitting only very small drinks of water to prevent further dehydration. Cubes of ice, melting slowly in a shallow dish, may be the best way of allowing a little fluid at a time to the dog.

The first foods fed should be fat-free to stop the liver discharging stored quantities of bile. Boiled chicken (removing the skin and fat under it) and rice or fish, egg, pasta can be tried.

Repeated vomiting (after investigation of the cause) can be treated with maropitant citrate as a once-daily dose that blocks the brain receptors known as NK-1; it is a prescription medicine.

A herbal approach is to use ginger; the fresh root has been used as an anti-emetic. A tincture of zingiber, which will keep for six months, is an alternative.

Dogs with dilated oesophagus can be kept nourished for life if the food is of the right consistency and fed from a raised level to assist gravity. Specific medication to reduce gastric acidity will be needed if there is an injury to the entrance of the stomach (such as when swallowing a sharp-edged bone that results in the stricture) or sometimes after a reflux of acid while the dog has had a general anaesthetic. Ballooning of a stricture may be attempted, or surgical exploration may be successful in opening up the oesophagus.

MALABSORPTION

This is a digestive problem where the dog may eat a lot of food, does not put on weight and has constant diarrhoea. The faeces are soft, greasy, large in quantity and have a rancid odour.

Malabsorption is not a specific disease but is often associated with shrinkage of the finger-like villi that are the main areas to absorb digested food. The dog is unable to use the masticated food that is soft and part digested, as it passes from the stomach into the small intestine. An overgrowth of bacteria that normally inhabit the tube of the small intestine can occur and the bacteria take the best of the nutrients, including vitamin B12. The TLI blood test

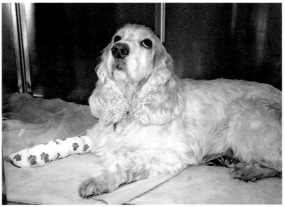

A Cocker Spaniel suffering from acute pancreatitis on a fluid therapy drip.

is very useful; supplementing the diet with pancreatic powder as an effective licensed treatment for non-specific diarrhoea may be advised.

PANCREATITIS

The pancreas is a hidden organ involved both in the control of blood sugar levels and in producing digestive enzymes. Unfortunately, self digestion by these enzymes (autolysis) often follows any inflammation of this organ once damaged. The acute condition is relatively uncommon in dogs, associated with a high-fat diet or injury. It can be a devastating disease: spontaneous illness of the deep-seated gland has been associated with the use of corticosteroids and obesity. The dog may vomit, have a tucked-up belly and adopt a 'prayer position' to try to relieve pain near the stomach. Collapse and shock are complications such as when peritonitis develops.

Chronic pancreatitis is a continual inflammation of the pancreas. The signs of weight loss, reduced appetite and abdominal pain are not easily recognised. Diagnostic tests, similar to those for acute pancreatitis, will be used.

Diabetes mellitus (see p. 73) may be anticipated if the insulin-producing cells have been damaged or reduced in numbers as a result of the pancreas being inflamed.

Treatment: Nothing should be given by mouth for three to five days traditionally, to stop digestion of the cells, but treatment of acute pancreatitis requires hospitalisation and treatment for shock with fluid drips. Some recent authorities suggest that fluids given by mouth for the first few days may help. Antibiotics, painkillers and a low-fat diet will be prescribed.

EXOCRINE PANCREATIC INSUFFICIENCY (EPI)

This is a particular problem in German Shepherd Dogs, who may show the illness before two years of age. It can also develop following a severe case of pancreatitis in other breeds of dog. Genetically, it is probably an autosomal resessive trait and can be bred out to some extent. The acinar cells of the pancreas are the ones that produce important enzymes that are needed to complete the digestion of food as it passes down the small intestine. Fat is poorly digested, so greasy faeces and a ravenous appetite (from lack of nutrients ready to absorb) are two important signs. Weight loss and coprophagia (eating faeces) are also signs of the inability to digest the food fully.

Blood tests confirm the diagnosis. Dietary management, using low-fat diet and supplements of pancreatic enzymes mixed in the food, can produce a good improvement.

THE LIVER – HEPATIC DISEASE

The liver is the largest organ of the body and, arguably, one of the most important processing centres. Tucked away beneath the dog's ribs on the right side, it is never seen or heard! The liver has enormous regenerative powders, so clinical signs such as 'yellow jaundice' will not be seen until 70-80 per cent of liver cells have been injured. The liver is particularly susceptible to poisons, as it acts as the main filter centre.

Signs: The signs at first may be vague: perhaps yellowish faeces, weight loss, increased thirst, occasional sickness and loss of appetite. The yellow-coloured bilious vomit may be one of the few indications to the owner that the dog has a liver! More serious is when the white of the eyes turn yellow, the hairless areas of skin have a distinct yellow tinge, and the urine becomes brownish-orange in colour. These are signs

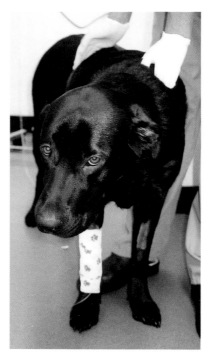

A Labrador Retriever attached to an intravenous drip stand receiving treatment for jaundice.

of jaundice (also called icterus), indicating that the capacity of the liver to get rid of the waste product bilirubin has become overstretched. Pale fatty faeces, fluid in the abdomen (ascites), and bleeding disorders (due to the inability to produce blood-clotting factors) will be seen as the disease progresses.

Causes: There are many causes, divided into sudden (acute) liver damage or more common chronic with a gradual onset of symptoms:

- Poisons and toxins. These may be drug-induced or toxins produced by bacteria and by

blue-green algae in water.
- Bacterial infection, such as leptospirosis, salmonella.
- Virus infection with infectious canine hepatitis (ICH) or from canine herpes.
- Acute pancreatitis or any bruising of internal abdominal injury.

Chronic onset may be due to:
- Cancer of liver or adjacent organs when secondary tumours reach the liver.
- Slow-acting drugs, often given for some other condition (e.g. phenobarbitone for fits).
- Immune-mediated, known as chronic progressive hepatitis.
- Inherited conditions, such as copper toxicity in Bedlington and other terriers, or porto-systemic shunts in Staffordshire Bull Terriers and others.

Liver failure is fortunately rare, but it produces some nasty side effects:
- Brain disturbances known as encephalopathy. This is when 70 per cent of liver function is lost, and ammonia in the blood stream reaches the brain, causing toxaemia and neurological signs. There may be aimless pacing, apparent blindness and general disorientation (head pressing in corners). The signs are worse after a meat meal, due to protein nitrogen waste; eventually, fits and coma may occur as the disease reaches the end point.
- Ascites or fluid in the abdomen

CONSTIPATION AND STRAINING

It is important to decide whether the infrequent or difficult defecation is due to the type of diet and lack of water or due to some internal obstruction of the intestine. A complete obstruction can be seen as straining with little or no faeces. Conditions such as an obstructed bladder, colitis or an ano-rectal tumour might be confused with simple constipation. Many middle-aged and older males have enlarged prostates that can first be recognised by the flattened ribbon faeces produced after prolonged straining. Bone chips, glass or metal fragments that are in the rectum could cause the dog to strain repeatedly, but it is then too painful for the faeces to pass through.

Dogs can become voluntarily constipated if well house trained and then have little opportunity for outdoor exercise. This presents a difficulty if the dog is taken on a journey or goes to a dog show with unfamiliar or threatening surroundings. A day or two without defecation is not a great concern, but, after that, faeces retained in the colon become hard and dry and are difficult to pass unless lubrication is supplied.

causes the swelling and hanging down of the 'stomach muscles'. It becomes pendulous and slows up the dog. The cause is a loss of protein in the blood due to liver dysfunction. Acites is also seen in some heart disease (see p. 81).

• Cirrhosis of the liver is scarring with fibrous tissue often associated with skin bruising and bleeding due to loss of essential blood-clotting factors.

Treatment: Good nursing and attention to diet are important. Dietary changes can take the digestive load off the liver. Nutritional support is available through special diets that have high-quality protein in moderation, careful use of fat as an energy source, and plenty of starch and fibre. Vitamin B and K supplements are needed, and a restriction on salt intake will also help. The vet may prescribe antibiotics, anti-inflammatories or use intravenous fluids in acute cases. Lactulose is used to help bind free ammonia in the blood.

DISORDERS OF THE RECTUM AND ANUS

CONSTIPATION & STRAINING
Treatment: In the short-term it is easy to administer mineral oil (liquid paraffin) by a syringe or dessertspoon in the mouth. Diet changes may be necessary as well as increasing fluid intake. Some of the 'geriatric' diets contain more suitable fibre to stimulate regular bowel activity. High levels of fibre are best if incorporated as a finely ground powder rather than left on top of normal food.

LICKING IN THE ANAL REGION
Rectal tumours can be removed surgically. More serious are cancerous tumours inside the rectum, which may only be found after internal examination by the vet, using a rubber finger stall to feel inside the rectum. This examination is also used to examine for blocked anal sacs (and for an enlarged prostate in male dogs).

BLOCKED ANAL SACS
There are a pair of anal pockets that contain greasy odorous fluid that are used by dogs to mark where they have deposited their

faeces. Territorial marking in this way is used by many wild animals (known as middening in badgers). On some diets, the sacs fail to be emptied at the time of depositing faeces from the rectum.

Anal sacs can become infected by bacteria or their exit canal can become blocked if the sac contents become waxy or semi-solid. Often a dog will attempt to relieve the irritation or unwittingly empty a full sac after sliding on any rough surface. This may be intentional when a carpet in a stranger's house is visited, especially if another dog has left smell traces.

Anal abscesses develop if the bacteria in the gland multiply. There is a painful swelling and then this is relieved when a hole adjacent to the anus appears and a gush of blood-stained fluid discharges. Bathing with salt water helps to clear any remaining fluid. The dog loses the pain immediately. It may be decided to seek antibiotic and analgesic treatment from the vet until the hole closes up. Repeated abscesses cause scarring and the possibility of narrowing known as anal stricture.

Treatment: Avoid the sacs becoming blocked and there will

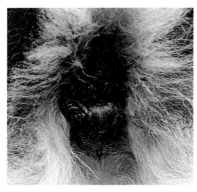

Anal furunculosis: The German Shepherd Dog has a tendency to develop this condition.

be no need for antibiotics. Diet containing more bulk or fibre will help a dog to empty the sac contents a little at a time. If the dog loses weight, the muscles of the perinaeum become less flabby and will help in the natural emptying process.

Some owners take their dog regularly to the vet to have the sacs emptied by squeezing them either internally or externally, catching the contents in a pad of cotton wool. A veterinary nurse may instruct the dog owner how to do this procedure: it is usual to elevate the dog's tail to slightly evert the anus. Then, using the fingers of one hand spread out, press upwards and slightly inwardly until the fluid contents are felt coming out on to the pad made ready.

Plenty of exercise for the dog tones up the muscles and frequent opportunities to defecate aids the empting of the sacs a little each time.

ANAL FURUNCULOSIS
This is a painful condition, mainly in German Shepherd Dogs but it is found in other breeds too. It is characterised by deep skin ulcers around the anus on the skin, known as the perineal region. Constipation and straining may be due to pain and discomfort; the holes may ooze and bleed.

Cause: It is not fully understood, as there is a breed predisposition and it is thought there must be some immunity failure. It is also associated with dietary intolerance, colitis and autoimmune disease (see p. 124).

Treatment: Surgical treatment has been successful and freezing with liquid nitrogen was also popular for many years. Treatment of the immune disorder using ciclosporin as a potent immunosuppressant has produced excellent results in some patients, but ask your vet what is best! Tablets need to be given twice-daily for eight weeks and more than 60 per cent of dogs need no further treatment.

THE KIDNEYS AND URINARY DISORDERS

Chapter 9

PART II

The main functions of the kidneys are to remove excess fluid and waste products from the body. The kidneys receive a quarter of the blood pumped out of the heart and are one of the vital organs of the body. There are other important functions, such as maintaining the correct degree of alkalinity, and maintaining the balance of electrolytes and hormones associated with red blood production. In the kidney, the blood is filtered through the nephrons (a basic filter unit; there are thousands of nephrons in each kidney). The first filtration through the nephrons produces a very watery fluid. As this passes through the little tubes within the kidney, it becomes more concentrated, since water is progressively reabsorbed and further waste products can be added. Then the

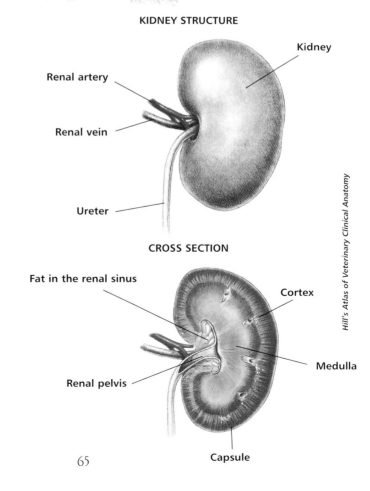

KIDNEY STRUCTURE

Kidney

Renal artery

Renal vein

Ureter

CROSS SECTION

Fat in the renal sinus

Cortex

Renal pelvis

Medulla

Capsule

Hill's Atlas of Veterinary Clinical Anatomy

THE URINARY SYSTEM

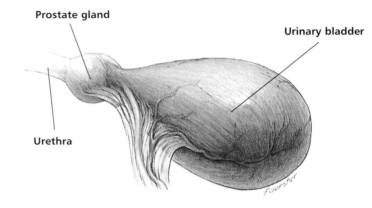

Prostate gland

Urinary bladder

Urethra

urine passes down to the bladder for temporary storage as urine.

The decision to empty the bladder is under conscious control of the brain. Once a puppy develops, it is 'house trained' (rather than automatically emptying its bladder when near full). These features of urine formation and bladder control can lead to unpleasant symptoms when the kidney and control mechanism is disturbed. Some of the signs you might see when there is a urinary disorder are described.

URINE DISORDERS

BLOOD-STAINED OR DISCOLOURED URINE

The colour of the urine may not be noticed if the dog is used to going outside on grass or some other absorbent surface. This is even more probable with a bitch who urinates close to the ground. Every year, if snow lies on the ground, reports of blood in the urine are made to veterinary surgeons. Chilling of the abdomen, especially in short-legged dogs, may be a factor, but the colour of the urine passed makes a contrast against the whiteness of the snow.

Causes: Abnormality of the urine can be a clue to causes:

• Red or red-brown colouration indicates that red blood cells have got into the urine after injury or disease. The pigments haemoglobin (from the red blood cells) and myoglobin (from muscles) also colour the urine. Blood in the urine, known as haematuria, may appear in the first part of the urine stream. This suggests that the problem is near the 'outlet' (e.g. the penis, prostate gland, or urethra, or the vagina or uterus of the female). Blood that appears towards the end of the stream suggests it is from the bladder lining or the prostate. If the blood becomes mixed in with all of the urine passed, it may originate from the kidneys, bladder or the connecting tubes. Vaginal bleeding before the end of the heat may be mistaken for disease, but if it is mucoid in character – and during oestrus – it is quite normal.

• Yellow urine indicates liver disease where the excess bile pigments are being removed as fast as possible. The yellow-orange bilirubin is carried in the blood, but in jaundice the excess pigment colours the skin and the urine. This can happen after the abnormal destruction of red blood cells (haemolytic jaundice) with the release of haemoglobin, which has to be

AGEING AND FAILING MEMORY

It is not uncommon that the older dog will be less alert and appears to have a failure of memory. The learned behaviour of being 'house clean' can diminish and result in the deposit of faeces or urine at unexpected sites when the dog is not under supervision. This condition, known as cognitive dysfunction syndrome, may be thought of as similar to senile dementia in humans.

Careful examination of the elderly dog or bitch is required, as diabetes mellitus, Cushing's syndrome, a pituitary tumour, hyperparathyroidism, an obstructed bladder, kidney failure or pyometra in the bitch are all possible causes of urine being produced frequently and deposited just where the dog happens to be.

Supervision and medication to help brain function may be beneficial. It is also possible that arthritis (making a dog slow to get up and move) may make a dog unable to get to his usual place when he wants to relieve himself. Reward training, with praise or titbits, should be used at times when the dog empties his bladder or bowels at the correct place.

processed by the liver.
- Dark yellow to orange colour is associated with fevers and/or fluid deficits after vomiting and diarrhoea with dehydration.
- Some medication and dyestuffs can colour the urine. Fluorescent green urine, due to artificial food colouring, has been seen.
- Urine that is browny-yellow and that produces a foam when shaken indicates that bile pigments from the liver are probably present. The vet will want to make further tests to confirm which diseases are causing these colour changes.
- A foul odour may suggest excess protein in the urine, as with cystitis; a sweet, fruity smell may indicate the presence of ketones, as in diabetes mellitus.

The smell of the urine may be very strong in diseases such as cystitis, as bacteria break down the urine in the bladder with the release of ammonia gas, but this also happens in old samples of healthy dogs.

Diabetic dogs have sugar in the urine, attractive to flies, but if the dog is untreated and becomes ketotic, the smell of acetone or pear drops may be detected, indicating the need for urgent treatment.

Treatment: Treatment depends on the underlying cause, but, in most cases, encouraging the dog to drink more will help to wash harmful substances away. The vet will prescribe treatment and the correct diet once a diagnosis has been made.

DRIBBLING URINE, INCONTINENCE

Incontinent dogs may have lost voluntary control of their bladder emptying and should not be punished. At first they have accidents where they have been sleeping, as the muscle at the exit to the bladder gets weaker if the dog is not conscious or sometimes mistakes are made in the house after having previously been 'house clean'. Passing urine when excited or distressed is another sign of weak control, but the submissive puppy or sometimes adult dog will roll on his back and

Drinking more than usual may be a sign of kidney disease.

produce a few drops of urine as a sign to another dog that he or she will remain subordinate. Stress incontinence, another cause of dribbling, can be treated with drugs that increase the muscle tone at the exit of the bladder.

When out on a walk, the frequent stopping by a dog to pass urine and the dribbling of small amounts of urine may indicate that a bitch is coming into season or a male dog may be aware of such a dog nearby and is marking out his territory with his urine smells.

Causes: A number of diseases may cause incontinence and tests at the surgery (including X-rays and scans) may be needed.
- Hormone imbalance may contribute to incontinence in neutered males or females. Treatment with supplements of hormones as well as drugs to increase bladder muscle tone will help. If incontinence after a spaying operation develops, it could be due to post-operative pelvic adhesions or cystitis.
- Neurogenic incontinence is the name given where there has been an interference with the nerve supply to the bladder. Causes such as injuries to the spine after a road accident or a kick, tumours, infections and inherited nerve weakness disorders can all affect the nerve supply to the bladder. In spinal paralysis the bladder fills slowly to full capacity then the pressure inside causes the overflow to trickle out, leading to intermittent, uncontrolled passing of urine.
- In spinal paralysis, the bladder fills slowly and then the pressure inside causes the overflow to trickle out, leading to the intermittent passing of urine and scalding of the perineum skin.
- A similar appearance occurs where the outlet to the bladder is blocked, most commonly by a mineral concretion known as 'the stone', although there may be many small stones or calculi.
- Tumours, such as bladder papilloma or stricture from injury, may be other reasons. Usually the dog will strain repeatedly and only a small quantity of urine can get through, but this may suggest incontinence, particularly if the dog has been left indoors on his own before little pools of urine are found round the house. The treatment of the over-distended bladder is by diagnosing the cause and correcting the type of obstruction present.

Dogs with kidney disease, as described below, will produce large quantities of watery urine. They are unable to concentrate their urine (a similar failure in diabetic dogs), which may be seen as incontinence in the house, if affected dogs do not have free access to the outdoors.

Treatment: The vet may use phenylpropanolamine or oestrogen if the bladder sphincter muscles are weak. Cystitis requires antibiotics whilst exploratory investigations and surgery may be required for obstructions or tumours.

DRINKING MORE THAN USUAL

Drinking more than usual can be a sign of kidney disease or another internal organ problem. Diabetes, liver disease, pituitary tumour, and over-salted foods can all produce excessive thirst and then urine output.

Water consumption of less than 60 ml/kilogram/day is considered normal. Weigh the dog and measure the volume of the usual drinking bowl. Check if the dog drinks at other places too. Most moist or wet diets provide quite a lot of water through their content; dry diets may contain as little as 6-10 per cent water.

STRAINING TO PASS URINE

Difficulty and pain in passing urine is known as dysuria.

Causes:
- Cystitis – an inflammation of the bladder lining
- Prostate disease in uncastrated males
- Bladder stones (calculi)
- Tumours

CYSTITIS

The signs are frequent and painful urination. The urine may appear cloudy or have blood traces and a pungent odour. Culture of samples of urine caught in a dish is not reliable due to the risk of contamination, as the urine has passed through genital-tract resident bacteria. Urine collected with a catheter should be analysed, as this can be tested for bacteria, white blood cells and protein. The

HEALTHY LOWER URINARY SYSTEM

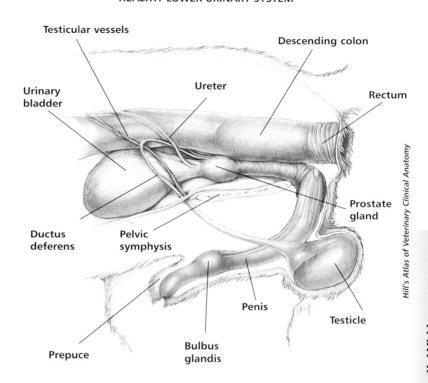

Testicular vessels · Descending colon · Urinary bladder · Ureter · Rectum · Ductus deferens · Pelvic symphysis · Prostate gland · Penis · Testicle · Prepuce · Bulbus glandis

Hill's Atlas of Veterinary Clinical Anatomy

'gold standard' method is to obtain a urine specimen by cystocentesis (by directly puncturing the bladder and sucking out a sample with a sterile syringe). Fluid intake should be encouraged to get a good wash through and an appropriate antibiotic will usually be prescribed, based on the culture of the sample. A broad-spectrum antibiotic may first be used until culture results are obtained after a few days when a specific drug is chosen.

BLADDER STONES

A dog that does not pass urine freely but has prolonged squatting or leg lifting is likely to have an internal obstruction of the bladder, usually due to 'bladder stones' (calculi); more rarely, a tumour may obstruct the bladder exit. Calculi are pieces of gravel-like chalky substance. Some are 'jack shaped' or spiky, or, in some bitches, they are round, smooth objects that lodge in the bladder.

The stones are composed of various combinations of minerals and organic materials. Phosphates crystallise in stagnant alkaline urine, and when combined with magnesium and ammonia, they are known as struvite calculi. Other calculi, on

PART II

URINATING AT INAPPROPRIATE TIMES OR PLACES

The voiding of urine is not always done because the bladder has filled 'to the brim'. Any form of irritation or increased sensitivity in parts of the urinary tract may make the dog want to stop and pass urine.

Causes:
• Behaviour problems need investigating
• Bladder abnormality – ectopic ureter in puppies
• Poisoning with kidney irritants
• Liver failure
• Diabetes mellitus
• Diabetes insipidus
• Cushing's syndrome
• Pituitary tumour
• Hyperparathyroidism
• Kidney failure
• Pyometra in unsprayed bitches
• Cystitis

Treatment: The treatment of inappropriate urination requires a thorough examination and a diagnosis by the vet before a behaviour therapist is consulted. Over-frequent and inappropriate urination may be a sign of poisoning as the kidneys attempt to remove toxic substances, rat poisons or even chocolate. Diabetes mellitus, a pituitary tumour, an obstructed bladder, or kidney failure are all possible causes of urine being produced frequently and deposited just where the dog happens to be. Behaviour retraining will not help.

Careful examination of the elderly dog or bitch is needed to eliminate some of the possible causes listed above; there are some medications that can be used to help the bladder sphincter muscle to function better.

Reward training when eliminating out of doors is advised, while ignoring the dog if an 'accidental spill' occurs. In all cases, it is important not to chastise the dog when a pool of urine is found in the home or indoors elsewhere. To make any sense, the verbal reprimand must be given just as the urine begins to flow and the dog is led to an alternative place to go out of doors, but this is seldom possible. Even a delay of a few minutes will mean that the dog does not connect what he is receiving punishment for; the dog will tend to hide away, which can make retraining even more difficult.

analysis, are found to be composed of calcium oxalate, cystine (as an inherited defect) or ammonium urate (mainly in Dalmatians).

Any of these crystals can cause more frequent urination or can totally obstruct the urethra on occasions, with constant strainings but with little or no urine passed.

Treatment: Internal examinations, X-rays and endoscopy may be needed to make a definite diagnosis and chemical analysis of the stones will help to decide the best treatment. Some calculi can be dissolved by adjusting the diet and increasing water intake, but many can only be removed by surgical operations.

Cystotomy is a relatively simple operation to open up and scoop out the bladder contents. Sometimes the calculi are well down the bladder neck, and catheters to flush through are required. The dog will be encouraged to drink more after the operation, as there is a tendency for bladder stones to reform.

LICKING AT PENIS

Unfortunately a straw-coloured penile discharge is not uncommon in some entire male dogs and it can also occur in castrated dogs.

Infection of the tip of the penis and prepuce is known as balanoposthitis. It is usually more of an inconvenience to the dog (and aesthetically distressing to the owners) than a serious disease. A copious green discharge causes the dog to lick, to try to keep clean, but there is the risk of skin ulceration and bleeding.

Causes:
- Herpes virus has been associated with a chronic sheath infection and small blisters can be identified sometimes
- Urethritis
- Ulcers from licking
- Grass seeds and awns can get into the prepuce. In rare situations these awns can then track under the skin and produce a fluid swelling as far away as the skin fold at the front of the knee. To search for such foreign bodies, it is quite easy to extrude the flaccid penis to inspect for any foreign matter, as the bone within the penis, the os penis, stiffens the base of the penis.

Treatment: Treatment may involve syringing out the prepuce with a mild disinfectant or, after swabs for culture have been taken, an appropriate antibiotic may be prescribed.

LICKING AT THE VULVA

Excess licking under the tail by the bitch might indicate cystitis or urethritis irritation. A vaginal discharge may not be visible, but the hairs around the vulva may be sticky or matted.

Causes:
- Pyometra in the unspayed bitch causes mucoid fluid to leak from the uterus in the 'open' discharging disease. A copious blood-tinged discharge causes the dog to lick.
- Onset of heat or oestrus is seen first by the bitch paying particular care to her toileting. It should also be remembered that the bitch with impacted anal sacs will lick around or chew at the region and it may be confused with a bitch licking the vulva area.
- Tumours can cause irritation and may eventually protrude to the outside after excessive licking at the vulva. Neoplasm growths of the vulva are rare but tend to be aggressive carcinomas.
- Herpes virus may cause blisters just inside the vulva.
- Urethritis – the urethra from the bladder exits on the floor of the vagina. Bacteria may be present.

Treatment: Once a cause has been discovered, antibiotics may be used. With tumours, surgical removal of the mass is usually successful. Treatment for chronic infections in the bitch can be given using probiotics by mouth and syringing the vagina with unpasteurised yoghurt to help to colonise the interior with healthy organisms.

KIDNEY DISEASE

Renal disorders include the various forms of nephritis and may be seen as acute renal failure or, more often, the slow development of a loss of kidney function. Disease involves changes in the filter units known as nephrons and it is more accurate to speak of nephrosis since there is not always an inflammation of the kidney. There are thousands of these filter units and it is only when 75 per cent have been destroyed that kidney failure (uraemia) sets in.

KIDNEY FAILURE

The signs to look for are:
- Foul breath
- Discoloured/loose teeth
- Loss of appetite and weight
- Increased drinking suggested by an empty water bowl
- Noticeably long drinks with an output soon afterwards of large quantities of watery urine
- Very pale urine, which, when tested, has a low specific gravity, containing protein and damaged cells from the kidney.

If left untreated, advanced kidney failure, with increased thirst, progresses to dehydration, as the dog may start to vomit and gastric ulcers can develop; anaemia occurs from loss of vomited blood and the depression of the bone marrow that forms replacement red blood cells.

PART II

SPECIFIC TYPES OF RENAL DISEASE

The nephritic syndrome:
This is a special type of kidney disease that is either immune-mediated damage inside the nephrons or from a clogging up of the filters with amyloid (a starch-like protein). Ascites (fluid under the skin) and fluid in the chest (known as hydrothorax) are additional signs to those of chronic renal failure, as large amounts of protein are lost in the urine.

Pyelo-nephritis: This is usually caused by an infection that moves in to the kidneys from the bladder. Diseases with infection such as pyometra and cystitis may spread up the ureters to reach the kidneys. The painful stiff-legged gait and arched back are typical signs of the disease and the dog will seem very ill. Urgent treatment with antibiotics after urine culture is necessary to stop the dog having chronic pyelo-nephritis with weight loss, loss of appetite and excessive thirst and urine output. It may be necessary to operate and remove such a kidney.

Glomerular nephritis: This is yet another type of kidney disease in which the kidney units become clogged with protein produced by the dog's own antibody system. There is a hereditary tendency in

CHRONIC RENAL DISEASE

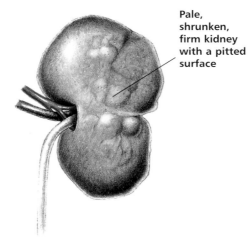

Pale, shrunken, firm kidney with a pitted surface

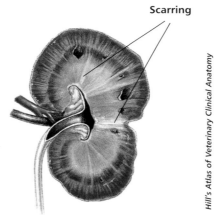

Scarring

Hill's Atlas of Veterinary Clinical Anatomy

Dobermanns, Samoyeds and Bull Terriers, as a congenital disease in puppies or as an immune response to adult infections. A large quantity of protein is lost in the urine, puppies have a large appetite but they become thin with a protruding spine and develop a swollen abdomen from the ascites.

Treatments: In general, the treatment for these kidney

disorders includes feeding special diet foods to try to ease the load on the damaged kidneys. Diet supplements with vitamins may be given, and, for some dogs, a low-phosphate diet will be given to stop the bones becoming soft ('rubber jaw' is an advanced sign of disease). Aluminium antacids will often help to control vomiting and absorb excess phosphorous in the diet given.

Antibiotics will be used in some cases and often any anaemia will have to be corrected as well. Blood and urine tests repeated at intervals will need to be taken to monitor progress. Vets will use fluid therapy: a flow of 2ml/kg/hour of urine is aimed at, and diuretic drugs may be used to improve the flow.

DIABETES

Diabetes exists in two forms. The commonest, known as sugar diabetes or diabetes mellitus (DM), is described on p. 73. Found in older dogs, there is a tendency to overeat and become fat.

DIABETES INSIPIDUS (WATER DIABETES)

The less usual diabetic condition, known as diabetes insipidus, is caused by a hormone failure of the pituitary gland. The kidneys are involved in the type known as central form or nephrogenic form, where the collecting ducts in the kidney fail to respond to the hormone. The filtration by the kidneys is controlled by antidiuretic hormone ADH secreted in the pituitary gland. The more ADH is released, the more water is taken back into the body and the less quantity of urine is formed in the healthy dog. If there is a pituitary tumour or other cause, not enough ADH is released, so a large proportion of the water first filtered by the kidneys is not reabsorbed but passes out as weak urine. The dog correspondingly must drink more to make up for the loss of fluid in the urine. If confined to the house or even overnight, the dog's bladder may have filled up in a short time and the bladder is emptied in an uncontrolled way.

Treatment: Tests as an inpatient at a veterinary hospital or clinic can be used to diagnose this type of diabetes: tests are known as the water deprivation test and the ADH response test. Treatment is successful and hormone medication as a replacement is possible: nose drops can be used or a thiazide diuretic for the nephrogenic form, depending on availability.

DIABETES MELLITUS

This is not a kidney disease but the signs you are most likely to see are of passing increased volumes of urine, so it can be included here for consideration. The increased thirst and weight loss are other leading signs of this endocrine (hormone) disease, which is caused by a lack of

insulin. Many overweight dogs become diabetic, so the daily calorie requirement needs to be measured. Female diabetic dogs become much worse at each heat, as progesterone (one of the hormones produced) blocks some of the effect of insulin. Spaying will be advised to prevent the insulin fluctuating. Such surgical operations are safe as long as the bitch is stabilised on insulin.

Diabetes is associated with a deficiency of the insulin hormone produced by the pancreas or it may be due to an insulin resistance, as with cases of obesity. The disease is not uncommon and between 1 in 200 and 1 in 800 dogs and bitches may be affected. Female dogs are twice as often affected as their male counterparts, there is a familial trend and certain breeds are more commonly affected than others (e.g. the Miniature Poodle).

In type 1 diabetes, it is the beta cells of the pancreas that are attacked, probably as an autoimmune reaction, so that when three-quarters of the cells are destroyed the rest can no longer produce enough insulin. The early signs of increased blood sugar may be hardly noticed by a dog owner, but when this amount has been destroyed, the signs can develop abruptly.

In type 2 diabetes, the cells become resistant to the action of insulin in storing blood sugar. This is most often found in fat dogs but has been found after prolonged glucocorticoid (steroid) medication, with some heat

A diabetic dog being given an insulin injection administered by his owner.

control hormones (progestagens) and with pituitary tumours.

Signs: The signs to look out for in diabetes are:
- Increased thirst
- Increased urine output
- Increased appetite
- Severe loss of weight
- Tiredness and loss of energy
- The weight loss may not be noticed at first in an overweight dog, especially if an attempt to diet has been made. Later on, dogs with high sugar levels may develop eye cataracts and may lose their sight.

Treatment: The aim of treating a diabetic dog is to avoid these complications by regulating the level of sugar in the blood. Management of the dog will involve insulin injections, since drugs given as tablets are not so effective in dogs. Diet control and correction or prevention of cases of insulin resistance may be needed.

PART II

PART II

Type 3 diabetes can result from overeating or from an excess of hormones. Glucocorticoid hormones (GCH) are produced excessively by the adrenal glands of stressed dogs and this can add to a diabetic's problems. Cortisol is a hormone associated with stress and it helps in releasing more glucose into the blood in preparation for activity following a stressful encounter.

The vet will make tests and decide on the type of insulin to use and when it has to be injected. The insulin must be injected at a proper carefully calculated dose level and at a fixed time. If a 'Lente' insulin is used, this should last long enough to inject once a day. There is now a tendency to advise two daily doses of an intermediate acting type (NPH or Lente), given as half the dose at 12-hour intervals. In some cases this is thought to better stabilise the blood levels. The vet will advise you of the most suitable protocol and it will depend on the availability of someone in the home being able to administer injections at set times. This will be a 365-days-a-year routine, so a second person should be trained for any absences through holidays or human illness.

Diet is also very important. Sufficient protein is needed to maintain body weight, but carbohydrate (biscuits etc.) must be limited in the diet. Anything that floods the blood stream with sugar is avoided. Special diets may be purchased as canned or dried products where the carbohydrate is only 55-60 per cent of the energy intake. Dietary fibre is added to decrease the requirement for insulin, as the added fibre means that emptying of the stomach after a meal is slower. When the passage of food down the intestines is slowed, it has the effect of also slowing the sugar absorption. A mixture of soluble fibre (such as oats and beet pulp) is needed along with insoluble fibre (such as cellulose); pea haulm fibre is beneficial.

Generally, the food should be offered before an insulin injection is made. Two meals can be given – the second after eight hours if a single dose is advised. Where two injections are necessary, the food has to be divided into four equal portions, one at each injection time and the second fed six hours later. This can present timing problems and adjustments made to the schedule may be tried unless the vet recommended a specific timetable.

If the dog goes off his food, the amount of insulin injected may have to be temporarily reduced. Your vet will advise you in detail about what you should do. Do not attempt to alter the dose of insulin until you have reported the problem. If a dog is left untreated, the body systems resort to using fat as a source of energy; fatty acids are released faster than can be dealt with. This will lead to ketones appearing in the blood, causing toxicity that is seen as vomiting, a sweet breath odour, loss of appetite, dehydration and an impending death from ketoacidosis. Urgent treatment with fluid therapy, as well as soluble insulin given intravenously, is a necessity at this stage. Glucose and electrolyte levels will need monitoring frequently.

All diabetic dogs receiving insulin by injection need periodic measuring.

Most dog owners may be advised to monitor the sugar in the urine. This can easily be done using Dipstix (a test obtained from the vet). This test on the urine may only have to be done once a week if the patient is stabilised, but results should be written down in a 'diabetic diary'. Where unusual swings from high to low sugar are seen, further blood tests may be needed to create a glucose curve. This involves serial blood tests often taken every two hours over a day's observation period.

The advice given by your vet on insulin injecting may be on these lines:

- Increase the insulin dose by two units if the urine dipstick reads glucose 2+ or above
- Maintain the same insulin rate for injection of only 1+ above
- Reduce the insulin dose by two units if the sample reads negative for glucose.

Remember, obese animals should lose weight. Bitches should be spayed as soon as they are stabilised on insulin, as the hormones during a heat greatly disrupt the insulin dependence of the body.

HEART AND LUNG PROBLEMS

10 Chapter

The cardiovascular system (involving the heart and blood vessels) and the respiratory system (involved in breathing) will be covered as one subject since the signs of illness with one system are not dissimilar with the signs of the other. Coughing is an example of a common symptom. Bluish gums or lips have been described under mouth signs, but should be mentioned here again as an important sign of heart or breathing failure.

BREATHING ABNORMALITIES

Dogs breathe at a normal rate but will start panting if excited or if the temperature rises. It is important to keep the mouth moist by allowing access to water, as this is the main cooling mechanism for a dog. When breathing becomes forced or the dog breathes more quickly than usual while resting, then consider if there could be a heart or lung problem. Breathing at a faster rate than 30 breaths a minute indicates pain, fever or anxiety, but the more forced expirations at a quicker rate indicate disease. Breathing through an opened mouth rather than through the nose in the resting dog should also be noted as an abnormality.

Causes:
- Infections – often a virus
- Congestive heart failure – the colour of the lips and tongue should be noted (see p. 52 Mouth)
- Pneumonia or bronchitis – due to bacteria or even roundworm migration
- Lung tumours or those around the heart – there is usually a progressive loss of weight and appetite
- Heat stroke – hyperthermia
- Shock
- Any airway obstruction or collapsed lung (pneumothorax)

Other causes of rapid laboured breathing are poisoning, such as Paraquat, gastric torsion (see p. 59), dehydration, and diabetes ketoacidosis.

Treatment: Any acute distress in breathing is an immediate life-threatening emergency. Oxygen therapy may be called for, but this can only be safely used in veterinary premises. Tight-fitting collars and jackets must be removed. Usually it is first necessary to find out why a dog is showing distress before using specific treatment.

BREATHING NOISILY OR WITH OBSTRUCTED SOUNDS

The commonest breathing noise is when the dog is asleep –

STRUCTURE OF THE HEART

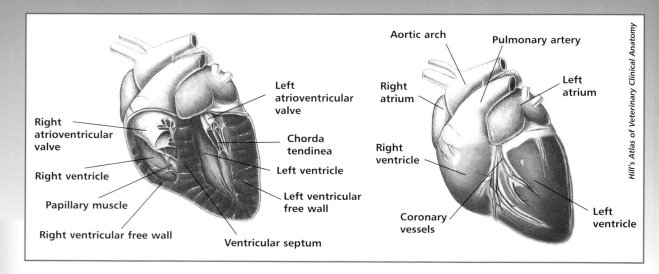

Aortic arch

Pulmonary artery

Right atrium

Left atrium

Left atrioventricular valve

Right atrioventricular valve

Right ventricle

Chorda tendinea

Left ventricle

Papillary muscle

Left ventricular free wall

Right ventricular free wall

Ventricular septum

Coronary vessels

Left ventricle

Hill's Atlas of Veterinary Clinical Anatomy

snoring may be loud enough to wake up humans in the same house! Snoring indicates a very relaxed, contented sleeping dog and the soft palate reverberates with each breath.

Causes:

- Laryngeal paralysis collapse of a fold of the larynx produces extreme gagging or 'roaring'
- An obese dog may be more likely to snore. Increasing daytime exercise can help to tighten up the muscles around the throat. Wheezing is more of a whistling sound, usually originating lower down than the throat as it is produced by narrowed bronchial tubes or in the windpipe
- Tracheal collapse (with a 'honking' type of noise) in middle-aged, obese dogs, especially Yorkshire Terriers

- Chronic bronchitis, such as caused by dust irritants or passive smoke inhalation, may cause such noises every time the dog breathes in or out
- Tumours in the larynx are rare but must be considered, as is any other similar obstruction in the trachea or lungs. Any nose blockage due to polyp tumours or collapsed nostrils may restrict the air as it passes in and out
- Inhaled foreign body (grass awn or a toy). A special sort of high-pitched rasping sound is known as stridor – it is louder and harsher than a wheeze. It may be heard only when the dog exercises. If it develops suddenly, it could be a foreign body in the larynx region, grass seeds and spiky leaves being troublesome if sucked into the throat.

CHOKING

The first thought when a dog is found choking or struggling to get his breath is that he must have something stuck in his throat.

ACCIDENTAL CHOKING

- There are rare occasions when a dog leaping for a tennis ball gets it across the back of the tongue and cannot get it out. As the ball gets stuck on to the larynx, the dog suffocates as he attempts to breathe in, but then, as the vacuum is released, some air can get back down to the lungs – and usually the dog comes round again. Such events need very urgent attention unless you are lucky enough to be able to push the ball forward with your fingers from outside while the dog relaxes as he is choked.

- A bone splinter is another possibility, but this will not cause so much choking. If the dog collapses, pull his tongue as far out as possible, then put your fingers in the mouth, sweeping them from one side to the other, and see if there is anything you can dislodge. Pieces of bamboo cane have been found, as well as spiky grass leaves. Do not push anything further down. Try a few thumps on the chest to get the exhaled air to force out an obstruction.

There are other causes that may lead to a dog appearing to choke.
- Oedema of the larynx is a fluid swelling possibly caused by an allergic reaction to an insect bite. The dog will become very distressed and urgent veterinary attention is needed, where effective medication will reduce the swelling that threatens to choke.
- Brachycephalic airway obstruction syndrome (BAOS) is the name given to obstructed breathing found in certain flat-faced, short-nosed breeds of dog. Any dog with a broad skull and short muzzle may be affected, but the Bulldog is the breed most likely to show these signs.
- An overlong soft palate may

UPPER AIRWAY

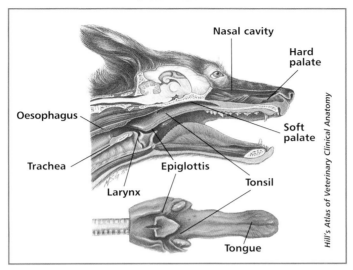

Hill's Atlas of Veterinary Clinical Anatomy

hang down on to the entrance to the larynx and the airway to the lungs.

Treatment: Removal of any foreign body is urgent.

Laryngeal paralysis, listed previously, is a distressing condition. When the dog breathes in, the laryngeal cartilages do not open and the vocal folds are not drawn open, the voice box producing a loud rasping noise. On breathing out, the cartilages and folds almost close, and the dog's bark becomes progressively weaker. Paralysis may result from injury (due to a swallowed ball or a tight choke chain). There is also an autosomal dominant hereditary condition found in some breeds of dogs aged 12 months and older.

Larynx collapse can be corrected by a surgical tie-back procedure, an operation under general anaesthesia. A laryngoscope light will first show that the paralysed vocal cords near the larynx come together in the middle instead of being wide open.

Removal of worms is needed if the tracheal worm *Oslerus osleri* has been seen with an endoscope; immature roundworms migrate through the lungs, but these will not be seen and other tests are needed.

GAGGING
This sound is halfway between a choke and a cough. Typically it is caused by mucus in the back of the throat or around the larynx. It can also be caused by a foreign body, such as a sideways-on bone fragment or a small bouncy ball, neither of which stop air getting in or out of the lungs. A dog with a nose infection and sinusitis will have a drip of sticky mucus back into the throat that the dog attempts to swallow, but, if very sticky, the mucus will cause gagging too. The harsh dry kennel cough also may cause gagging (see p. 87). An unlikely but not to be forgotten cause of gagging is the paralytic form of rabies. The tongue hangs out, the dog is unable to swallow, and drooling, coughing, gagging or foaming at the mouth are leading signs.

PART II

THE THORAX

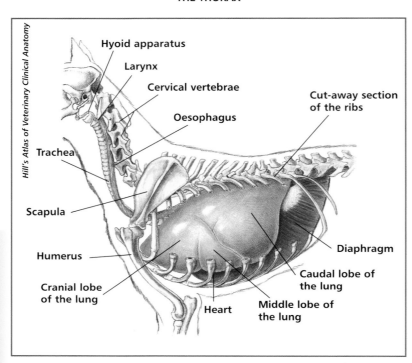

Hill's Atlas of Veterinary Clinical Anatomy

Hyoid apparatus
Larynx
Cervical vertebrae
Oesophagus
Cut-away section of the ribs
Trachea
Scapula
Humerus
Cranial lobe of the lung
Heart
Middle lobe of the lung
Caudal lobe of the lung
Diaphragm

PART II

GASPING, AFTER A ROAD ACCIDENT OR OTHER CHEST INJURY

If the rib cage becomes punctured after a dog fight or a road accident involves the ribs, air is sucked into the pleural space and the lungs partially or fully collapse. The emergency condition is called pneumothorax. This causes a breathing crisis, as, with each breath, more air comes in to shrink down the lung further. Another cause of pneumothorax is air escaping from the lungs, as with blunt injuries to the chest or bursting of air cavities in weakened lungs. The dog becomes ill quickly and urgent veterinary attention is needed.

The signs to look for are any respiratory distress after a chest injury that tends to get worse as the lungs collapse further. Forceful breathing is needed to draw air into the reduced-size lungs, and the blue colour of cyanosis will then develop.

Treatment: First-aid treatment is to bandage over any open chest wound using a moistened pad to help seal the chest. Dogs should be caged up, forcing them to rest. Air can be removed from the pleural space at the veterinary hospital by suction. In spontaneous pneumothorax, where the air leak is internal, suction is usually effective, but the operation of a thoracotomy operation may be needed to examine the lungs to find where the air leak is coming from.

SNEEZING

Explosive bouts indicate nose irritation; the forceful expulsion of air is intended to remove irritants from the nasal chambers. Allergies are not uncommon and sneezing with a watery discharge and pawing at the face is typically shown with canine atopy (p. 123). If violent sneezing is accompanied by head shaking and rubbing the one side of the face, consider a foreign body; a grass seed or awn can easily slip in past the opened nostril and then be difficult to dislodge. Sometimes a tiny piece of green remains at the nostril and, if fresh, the grass blade can be coaxed down out of the nose.

NASAL DISCHARGE

A small amount of mucus is needed to moisten the lining of the inner parts of the nose so that the remarkable scenting ability can work fully. Irritants, such as dust, pollen and fungal infections, may make the nose produce excessive amounts of mucus, often accompanied by sneezing. Nervous dogs may secrete a more clear, watery mucus that drips from the nose, a similar mechanism to when a dog salivates when seeing or smelling food.

A thick nose discharge will form a crust at the edge of the nostrils. This used to be a typical sign of distemper (see p. 89). A dog gets great relief when crusts

NOSE BLEEDING

A persistent nose bleed can be quite dramatic and blood may be found smeared on the walls and in pools on the floor, below the dog's face, if he has lain still. It is important to note whether the blood has clotted well, like blackcurrant jam, or whether it is pink and watery. This can help in deciding how to stop the blood loss. Sometimes the nose will bleed after a severe bout of sneezing, but at other times the nose may start dripping a little blood, which turns into a stream until the blood pressure falls so much that it almost ceases. An inherited condition known as von Willebrand's disease occurs in some breeds and there are other types of haemophilia found as well. It is difficult to apply any first-aid, such as an ice pack, and it may be best just to keep the dog as still and calm as possible until veterinary attention is available. Repeated nose bleeds will result in anaemia.

are gently soaked off and petroleum jelly (Vaseline) is applied to the area of the nostrils. A runny nose with an eye discharge and a cough is serious enough to visit the vet.

COUGHING

Two sorts of coughing should be distinguished by the dog's owner so that a report can be given to the veterinary surgeon. The productive cough is moister and deeper, bringing mucus up from the bronchii in the lungs (but unlike in humans, sputum is not often seen, as the dog swallows anything coming up into his mouth). The other type is much drier and is known as a non-productive cough. This is more like a constant tickle in the throat or lungs and a repeated coughing sound is made. For kennel cough the cough is very loud and honking in nature (see listing under Infectious Disease, p. 87).

Chronic bronchitis occurs in middle-aged and older dogs and will be diagnosed if a dog coughs for as long as a month or more without another cause being found. There is an inflammatory reaction of the breathing tubes inside the lung known as the bronchii. Dust and allergic causes are often suspected. The dog that sits at the kerb edge, waiting for a free passage to cross the road, may be unduly exposed to the particulate matter of diesel fumes, known to be a cause of human illness – and we breathe in high above the dog's nose level! The typical bronchitis cough is harsh, sounds dry, but eventually a little moist sputum may be brought up; any foamy saliva produced may be mistaken for a dog being sick.

Treatment: Treatment for such a cough involves removing irritants from the air; slightly moistening the air by using a steam kettle or a bowl of hot water may help. Overweight dogs have greater difficulty coughing, so a weight-reduction programme and gentle exercise may be part of the treatment.

Antibiotics may be used. There are a variety of products that suppress a cough or widen the breathing passages. Corticosteroids are also used at times: if there is a good response after three weeks, a lower maintenance dose may then be prescribed by the vet.

LUNG DISEASES

Coughing is one of the signs of pneumonia, an extremely serious condition that can be a cause of death.

PART II

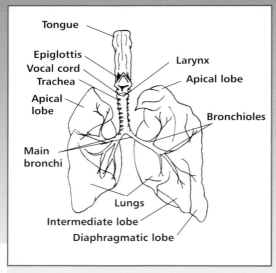

PATHWAY TO THE LUNGS

Labels: Tongue, Epiglottis, Vocal cord, Trachea, Apical lobe, Larynx, Apical lobe, Bronchioles, Main bronchi, Lungs, Intermediate lobe, Diaphragmatic lobe

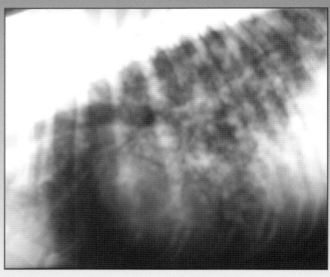

Chest X-ray showing secondary tumours in the lungs.

Causes: Pneumonia can be caused by bacteria, viruses, mycoplasma, fungal infections or by migrating worms. It is more common in young puppies and in older dogs. Dogs with severe pneumonia appear blue around the mouth and sit with their head and neck extended and elbows turned out. There may be mucus from the nose, a soft repeated cough, high temperature, rapid shallow breathing and a loss of appetite. Urgent veterinary attention is needed; medicines that suppress a cough should not be used.

Pleurisy is often used to describe a more severe lung infection. Bacteria that spread into the pleural space surrounding the lungs may cause fluid to accumulate. A pleural effusion can be an accumulation of blood or serum in the chest and the pressure collapses the spongy parts of the lungs, making breathing even more difficult.

A foreign body in the lungs is rare: grass seeds, barley awns or food material may get sucked down on inhalation and lodge in the finer breathing tubes. Sudden attacks of coughing after walking through a cornfield may only be an allergy, but if the condition remains for days or weeks, an investigation using bronchoscopy may be essential to find the cause. If examined within two weeks, the foreign body may be removable, but after that time it becomes encased in mucus and softens. Time for its absorption has to be given before the lungs return to normal.

Lung cancer is extremely uncommon and only accounts for about one per cent of all tumours that a dog may suffer from. It is a possibility that might be overlooked in the coughing dog, but X-rays or ultrasound scanning should help in the diagnosis. Secondary tumours can be expected after mammary tumours and others that spread through the blood stream. Osteosarcoma of bone, squamous cell and melanoma skin tumours frequently affect the lungs, known as metastasis.

COLLAPSING, STAGGERING OR FALLING

As well as from airway obstruction described above, heart disease can take several forms. It is commonest in the elderly, overweight dog.

HEART DISEASE

Causes:
- Congenital heart disease may be in the puppy from birth (congenital) but is quite rare
- Acquired as in a heart valve infection (endocardiosis). When the heart muscle is affected, it is known as myocardial disease
- Heart failure is the end stage of many heart conditions if untreated

When a dog collapses, heart disease is one of the most frequent causes. Only five per cent of heart cases are congenital, so middle-aged dogs may be at risk, even if appearing fit. When the dog is blue in the mouth and breathing heavily, it is likely to be a lung or respiratory blocked airway problem. But if the dog seems drowsy and the colour of the inside of the lips is pale or white, it usually suggests an internal heart 'attack' type of collapse. Human coronary heart disease attacks are rare in dogs. There is even uncertainty as to how often dogs have 'strokes' due to a cerebral haemorrhage. Some dogs showing signs associated with a stroke suffer from inner ear disease called vestibulitis, with loss of balance as the main sign.

It is necessary to consider the causes of collapse not involving the heart. When a dog is found collapsed, it may be difficult for the vet who sees the dog later to know the real cause of the dog's sudden attack. Careful observation at the time will help him to rule out other causes than the heart.
- Spinal problems, such as an embolism or a displaced disc, may cause a dog to collapse or drag his feet
- When a dog was normal then started struggling or throwing the legs at the beginning of the attack, it could be due to an epileptic-type seizure

CONGESTIVE HEART FAILURE

Breathlessness, disinclination to walk far, and frequent dry coughs may be associated with heart failure, especially in the older dog. The condition can arise when the heart is no longer able to maintain an adequate blood circulation for the body's needs. If the valves do not fully close after each heart beat, blood flows back rather than forwards towards the arteries. Depending on which valves are leaking, it may be the right side or the left side of the four-chambered heart that becomes overfilled with blood. With left-side heart failure it will be the lungs that pool with blood and the cough will be more marked; with right-side heart failure the jugular vein in the neck will be full and pulsate, and the liver swollen with venous blood will not function fully. Fluid will leak into the abdomen, causing the swelling known as ascites, or fluid may ooze into the chest cavity, causing lung problems similar to congestion within the lungs.

DILATED CARDIOMYOPATHY

When the heart muscle tires, it becomes overstretched with a reduced pumping ability of the right ventricle, which would normally be distributing oxygenated blood around the whole body. This condition is more common in the large or giant breeds and can lead to early death. As the heart muscle stretches, there is less strength and a decreasing forward flow of blood. Weight loss can occur in a few weeks, as appetite is

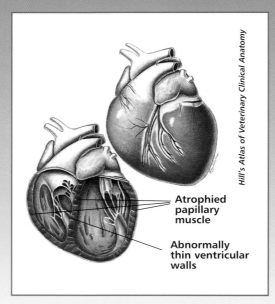

Hill's Atlas of Veterinary Clinical Anatomy

Atrophied papillary muscle

Abnormally thin ventricular walls

CANINE DILATED CARDIOMYOPATHY

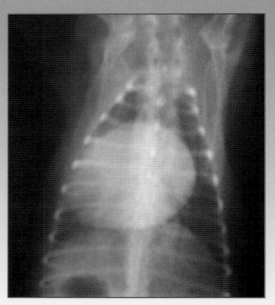

Chest X-ray showing a dilated heart (large globe shape).

depressed. Affected dogs are always tired, breathe rapidly, and cough frequently, sometimes producing blood in the sputum. Coughing at night is quite marked, unlike other coughs that occur after exercise. Sudden death may be anticipated if the condition is diagnosed.

HEART VALVE DISORDERS

Congenital valve disease in puppies is due to malformation, valve narrowing or abnormal openings between the two heart chambers. Most such dogs, unless operated on, die within the first years of life, and, because there is an inherited tendency, they must not be used for breeding. Heart murmurs may be heard in stressed dogs or when the blood is thin, as in anaemia. Such innocent murmurs usually correct themselves after re-examination.

Mitral or tricuspid valve disease (endocardiosis) in adults may result from a bacterial infection and are responsive to treatment. A heart murmur will be heard with a stethoscope. Dogs that are on cancer treatment (immunosuppressed) and on corticosteroids are at risk and more likely to get bacteria from the blood stream, settling on the heart valves and causing thickening and nodules. Dental procedures may allow mouth bacteria into the blood stream and antibiotics can be used at such times as a protective measure for the heart valves.

Murmurs are listened for with a stethoscope that indicate a leaking heart valve, but an electrocardiogram ECG or ultrasound may be used for greater accuracy. Not all murmurs are serious and can be heard if a dog is stressed or possibly anaemic, when the blood is thinner than normal. Puppies with murmurs under six months old may have 'innocent murmurs' that go as the dog matures. In all cases the dog needs to be watched and further tests to look for rhythm abnormalities may be needed.

Treatment: This will depend on the diagnosis. There are a wide range of medicines now available to treat most conditions. Each patient has to be assessed to decide on the severity of the disorder. Most dogs will benefit from carrying less weight. There are specific diets for heart disease: salt should be restricted and supplements containing arginine, taurine and carnitine may improve heart muscles. The long-term use of diuretics to remove fluid may be advised and loss of potassium from the body should be monitored.

HEARTWORMS

These worms live in the blood stream and block the upper heart chambers and blood supply to the lungs. The oxygen carried by the circulation to the rest of the body is restricted and an affected puppy may collapse and die. An adult dog with heartworms can produce millions of little worms in his blood, which may be sucked up by a biting mosquito as it feeds; later these larvae can be transferred to the next animal bitten by the mosquito. Only certain climate conditions suit these mosquitoes and the UK is still fairly free of heartworms. Early diagnosis and treatment should be given; it is very effective if given early enough, but always consult your veterinarian. A number of blood tests are available for heartworms. The most accurate is the heartworm antigen test; another test involves looking at the dog's blood under the microscope for minute worms in the microfilaria concentration test.

LUNGWORMS

These are uncommon in the UK, but it is best to be aware that, in southern parts of England, some puppies may get these special worms in the artery supplying the lungs, causing shortness of breath and coughing. A snail carries this worm as the intermediate stage of Angiostrongylus. Care should be taken with puppies in already infected areas when snails are about! (See also p. 24.)

ANAEMIA

Anaemia is the condition found with reduced amounts of haemoglobin, the oxygen-carrying protein within red the blood cells. The effects may be obvious after a dog has been seen to lose a quantity of blood. Tests results from the laboratory with a packed cell volume PCV of less than 37 indicates anaemia. The haemoglobin level should be greater than 12 G/dl in a healthy dog.

Causes: Anaemia may develop due to:
1. Bleeding after an accident or a deep cut or a nose bleed
2. Rupture of the spleen or other internal organ (liver or kidney)
3. Cancer where a tumour bursts (haemangiosarcoma)
4. Warfarin poisoning or blood-clotting disorder

Slow blood loss is more difficult to detect and may not be noticed until a lethargic dog is blood tested to look for anaemia.
1. Internal bleeding: This may be from the bladder when blood is seen in the urine or from the intestine where only blacker faeces than usual provides a clue. Stomach ulcer bleeding may be seen as blood in the vomit. Nose bleeds are obvious and may cause an acute bleeding episode. Warfarin poisoning causes blood leakages.
2. Parasites: Fleas and blood-sucking lice may be a cause. Hookworms in the intestine suck blood and will only be discovered if eggs are looked for in faeces. Babesiosis (rare in the UK) after tick bites introduce a parasite that destroys red blood cells.
3. Haemolytic anaemia: Where the body attacks its own blood cells as an auto-immune disorder.
4. Non-regenerative anaemias: Where the bone marrow is not capable of producing replacement cells.
5. Clotting disorders – von Willebrand factor, etc.

Treatment: Once the type of anaemia has been recognised, it may be decided to give a blood transfusion from a donor dog. Chemotherapy for cancer, immunosuppressive drugs for immune-mediated disease, or antibiotics for mycoplasma may be used. Vitamin B12 after a sudden blood loss can be injected, but there is less reason to give iron supplements or 'tonics' if the dog is a meat eater. Liver and kidney fed fresh may help the appetite and provide a source of replacement iron.

PART II

INFECTIOUS DISEASES, BACTERIA AND VIRUSES

11 Chapter

The dog, like all domesticated animals, can catch infections from being in close proximity to others of the same species, or may acquire infections from other animals, such as rats or even humans. Infections can be spread from one animal to another by saliva, by nose and cough droplets, in urine or faeces.

The major infections caused by viruses are largely preventable by the use of vaccines in puppy-hood. Animals can manufacture protective antibodies after exposure to a vaccine or after a natural, non-fatal infection. These antibodies circulate in the blood stream and can provide an immediate blocking response when an infection is again threatening the dog. There are also special cells in the immune

system called memory B lymphocytes, which allow for a quick response. Also, local immunity stops invasion of the body at the point of attack. The use of a kennel cough vaccine by applying drops of vaccine at one nostril is a good example of this.

The immune system has a protective role in animals, but, unfortunately, in a few disorders of dogs there is hypersensitivity of the immune system, which can cause skin diseases or disorders such as glomerular nephritis (see p. 72, kidneys) amongst others. Autoimmunity, where the body attacks itself, is one of the most dangerous of these over-responses. Healthy tissues can be destroyed by the immune system, as in haemolytic anaemia where red blood cells are broken down (p. 83 anaemia), in immune-mediated pancytopenia and in the skin disease known as pemphigus.

BACTERIA

Nasal discharge, loss of appetite, high temperature and possibly diarrhoea are the type of symptoms you may expect with bacterial diseases in the dog, but there is no clear-cut sign that distinguishes bacteria infections from virus infections – and often the two exist at the same time, making the dog more ill.

LEPTOSPIROSIS

A disease caused by the bacteria called spirochaetes, which are found in wild, as well as domestic, animals. These 'germs' are associated with moist places: they can live in stagnant water and are mainly spread through urine. Rats are one of the greatest threats as they often carry the disease and directly infect humans. Some dogs 'carry' the disease without looking ill and are a risk to other dog contacts. Water sources, soil,

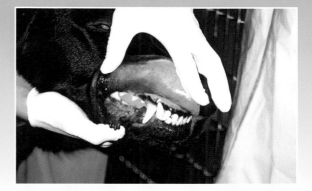

Yellowing of the white of the eye (left) and orange gums (right) in a dog suffering from jaundice as a result of Leptospirosis infection.

food or bedding may spread this organism; direct transmission is usually through broken skin, bite wounds or mucosal surfaces, such as lining of mouth or nose.

Signs: The blood vessels become damaged, most of the signs of illness are due to the destruction of the liver or kidney cells. The kidney is typically the first organ to be damaged, signs may include:

- Vomiting
- Fever
- Loss of appetite
- Dehydration and muscle pain
- Jaundice – this may appear later on as yellowing of the skin and eyeballs.

Treatment: Antibiotics and fluids can treat Leptospirosis successfully, but care is needed since there is the risk of spread to humans. The disease is zoonotic and humans too can die. Protective gloves must be worn when caring for infected dogs.

STREPTOCOCCAL INFECTIONS

These bacteria can cause sore throats, skin inflammations, and, in newborn puppies, death from septicaemia. As with most bacterial infections, antibiotics are used and the culture of swabs helps the vet to choose the most appropriate drug.

STAPHYLOCOCCAL INFECTIONS

These are more difficult to treat, as they can develop resistance to antibiotics. The infections commonly occur on skin, or as infections in the nose following damage caused by distemper virus. Swabs and sensitivity tests to choose the most appropriate antibiotic are advised. The vet will often need to start a course of antibiotics based on his previous experiences whilst awaiting the result of culture tests that may take a few days. When a staphylococcus affects the skin, the disease may be

called pyoderma. Furunculosis is a deep pyoderma.

BORRELIA BURGDORFERI

This organism causes Lyme disease (see p. 113). It is spread by tick bites, common in the USA and other tick areas but now becoming a greater a problem in the UK. A dog may show signs of sudden joint pain and stiffness, sometimes even weeks after a tick bite. Blood tests may be needed but after diagnosis antibiotics should be given for 2 to 4 weeks. There is greater awareness in people who are exposed to infection from tick bites, but the dog should not be blamed for the illness.

BORDETELLA

This organism is found in the trachea and bronchii of dogs affected with kennel cough. This contagious disease is heard first as a harsh dry cough, which may last for many weeks. Other causal agents of kennel cough include several different viruses,

PART II

mycoplasma and secondary bacteria (see p. 91).

BRUCELLA

This is a cause of infertility in bitches. It is not a real problem in the UK but may cause a problem with sterility and abortion in N. America. In France some breeders have resorted to the greater use of artificial insemination, to reduce the risk of transferable venereal diseases. The infected male dog may suffer from testicular degeneration too. With the greater global movement of dogs for breeding, owners intending to produce puppies should know of this risk.

CAMPYLOBACTERS

Campylobacters are the cause of infectious enteritis that distresses the dogs (and the owners who have to clean up the diarrhoea, especially if it has been voided indoors on the floor). Campylobacter often causes a fairly sudden and violent episode of diarrhoea.

Treatment: Usually involves fluid loss replacement either orally or by intravenous fluids, a smooth diet and possibly the use of antibiotics when in puppies.

COLIFORMS

These are bacteria associated with diarrhoea: some forms of E. Coli produce toxins that cause death of tissue. E. Coli can also be

Pseudomonas bacterial infection of a St Bernard with saliva-soaked skin (see below).

involved in urinary tract infections such as cystitis (see p. 69). E. coli strains from humans (mostly women) were found to be similar to those found in dogs with urinary tract infections. Enteropathogenic E. coli can cause severe illnesses in people as well as to companion animals.

PSEUDOMONAS

These are mobile bacteria often found in stagnant water. Some strains cause disease, especially at moist sites, such as the skin of the mouth, the urinary tract, the ear and any wounds.

SALMONELLAE

These are another cause of diarrhoea, usually less severe than Campylobacteriosis, but some dogs may become carriers and there is also the risk of transfer to humans. The risk is slight if normal hygiene precautions are observed, as in dealing with all diarrhoeas, such as thorough hand washing and disinfecting all the feed utensils after use.

Clostridia are another cause of bowel infection associated with colitis, often called 'antibiotic responsive colitis' but the disease can wax and wane unexpectedly.

TETANUS

Tetanus bacteria cause a disease that can develop in a patient after soil contaminates a wound. It causes the disease known as Lockjaw in humans. Fortunately, this is very rare in the dog, as the species has a natural resistance. A dog showing symptoms of sudden stiffness, developing weeks after a wound, should be examined. The vet would recognise tetanus signs which are characteristic. Immediate treatment with antibiotics and muscle relaxants should be given as soon as possible.

TUBERCULOSIS

As a bacterial infection it is most likely to be caught by a dog licking up the sputum of an infected human. In the last decade there have been more cases of 'open' human TB. Diagnosis is not readily made in dogs, as the signs are vague. Chest X-rays may be needed, but any dog living near an infected human should be closely watched.

Treatment: Treatment for tuberculosis is difficult, but strict isolation to stop the infection passing to other animals or people is a requirement.

PART II

BACTERIAL DISEASES

KENNEL COUGH

One of the most infectious conditions of the adult dog takes the form of a tracheitis in which droplets of mucus containing several infectious agents are coughed into the air. This means the infection is most likely to be spread at dog shows, boarding kennels, rescue centres and other places where dogs mix with each other. The condition was named 'kennel cough' but can be caught out of doors. However, most often it is the kennelled dogs who become ill.

Other factors, such as poor housing conditions and stress, may contribute to the disease developing. The infections spread readily when dogs are grouped together, either by direct contact or by air transmission.

Causes: The cause of kennel cough is a mixture of organisms including bacteria, viruses, Mycoplasma (which are normally found in the lungs but may become involved in the disease process) and possibly others. Any one of these on its own might cause a mild infection, but a combination of two or more may produce the debilitating disease sometimes lasting six weeks or more.

Dogs that are in close proximity, such as at a dog show, have a greater risk of being infected with Kennel Cough.

Signs: The severity of each attack depends on which of these infectious agents may be present, and the intensity of symptoms depends on which 'cocktail' mixture of pathogenic organisms predominates. However, the damage caused will invariably produce a deep cough as if there is something stuck in the windpipe.

It is not uncommon for pet dogs to show signs of a cough four or five days after attending gatherings with other dogs or being put into boarding kennels. Sneezing is also common in the early stages; a watery nasal discharge, which becomes thicker later, may also be seen. Milder cases are more troublesome to the humans than the dog, as a deep cough is brought on with excitement or exercise. Dogs recently fed may vomit, but the gagging and retching will eventually lead to some sticky mucus being brought up from the bronchial tubes. Often it is the owners and their neighbours who are more disturbed by the cough than the dog!

The dog's appetite remains good and most dogs seem bright and 'well'. It is rare for symptoms to progress to pneumonia, when there is laboured breathing and loss of appetite. There is a greater risk in older dogs, as the cough sometimes turns into more severe chronic bronchitis with a cough remaining for years. In this way some dogs become carriers and are a risk to others.

Treatment: Treatment with antibiotics may be prescribed, especially if there is the risk of pneumonia. A moist atmosphere to breathe, as produced by a steam kettle, has been used, but cough suppressant medicines and warmed soft feeds may be equally beneficial. In all cases a warm draft-free environment is needed to speed recovery. Pulling on the lead and any form of excitement are best avoided until all signs of

BACTERIAL ENTERITIS

Inflammation of the intestines may have a bacterial cause (see above); viruses and parasites too are involved. Bacteria normally live in the intestine running from the duodenum to the colon and are part of a healthy alimentary tract. Bacteria can cause gastrointestinal disease in a number of ways. Chapter 8 dealt with gastro-enteritis and its treatment. Infectious enteritis, often seen as diarrhoea with abdominal pain, can vary in intensity from severe haemorrhagic gastro-enteritis that can cause collapse and death to mild, loose faeces, which clears up with simple dietary treatment.

Treatment: Using antibiotics for bacterial enteritis is now discouraged due to the problem of leaving resistant organisms, which may then prolong the disease. Supportive treatment used will involve plenty of fluids, then a smooth 'bland' diet fed only after 24 hours of starvation. The fine cereal known as 'baby rice' is frequently advised by vets.

the cough have gone. You may be advised to use a chest harness or a 'Halti' head collar to reduce any pressure on the lower neck while exercising.

Kennel cough vaccines may help to prevent an attack and are often best given several weeks before it is planned to put a dog into boarding kennels or to take it to a show. There are two sorts of vaccine used: an injectable sort that contains inactivated cells or cell parts of *Brucella bronchiseptica* and the intranasal sort of vaccine. Such vaccines, used by placing drops in the nostril, give a quick protection and stimulate a local immunity as well as protecting against lung disease (see p. 18).

PERITONITIS

Abdominal pain may not be easily recognised but it can be one sign of an inflammation of the lining membrane of the abdominal cavity. As a disease it is most commonly associated with bacteria that have somehow leaked into or gained access to the abdomen.

Causes: Some of the most common causes are:
- Penetrating wounds into the abdomen
- Rupture of the bladder after a crush injury
- Leakage from the uterus in pyometra (see p. 105)
- Faulty surgical procedures (fortunately these are rare)

Signs: Dogs show pain in various ways: a tense facial expression, a reluctance to move and finding the coldest possible surface to lie on are warning signs. Vomiting may occur but often it becomes too painful for the dog to contract its abdominal muscles and vomit. Although peritonitis is fairly uncommon in dogs, it can be a cause of death.

The other signs of peritonitis are often vague and non-specific. There is usually a rise in body temperature, although it could be lower if in a state of shock. Blood samples are useful or the veterinary surgeon may take a sample of abdominal fluid in a technique known as abdominocentesis.

Treatment: Antibiotics and fluid therapy for any shock are often the first treatments used. A surgical exploratory operation may be needed to find out the cause of any underlying infection or to locate a defect. Washing the peritoneum with sterile fluids by 'lavage' and a peritoneal drain leading outside the body may follow a surgical operation.

VIRUSES

Viruses are extremely common in the dog population. Many cause only a mild illness but may be detected by taking blood tests that show the dog had a good protection through the response of its immune system. There are some really nasty viruses and these can best be avoided by using preventive vaccination. Rabies should be foremost of the horrible viruses that can infect a dog, but for puppies, the parvovirus that appeared in the early 1990s killed whole litters of unweaned puppies and then some that survived later dropped dead with heart failure. Distemper is almost a disease of previous centuries but could reappear at any time if vaccination is not used. Fortunately, all the vaccines available give a good protection against many of the viruses and these are recommended for initial use early in life (see p. 16).

Puppies aged between 6-12 weeks are most vulnerable to canine distemper.

ADENOVIRUSES

Adenoviruses come in two forms known as Type 1 and Type 2. Infectious canine hepatitis is the highly contagious disease caused by adenovirus 1. It is now rare but may occasionally be seen in unvaccinated and stray or homeless dogs still.

Signs: Most cases occur in puppies under 12 months of age and result in damage to the blood vessels, especially those supplying the liver and the kidneys. Tonsil enlargement and bleeding from the gums are outwardly visible signs and later a yellow (jaundice) colour may appear in the eyes. Most cases of hepatitis are now mild but in the severe form there is a high temperature and a lifeless dog, with a tucked-up abdomen and a desire to lie on a cold floor or stone surface. Bloody diarrhoea, collapse and a fairly quick death is the worst outcome. Some puppies that die after having fading puppy syndrome may have had hepatitis.

Treatment: As an acute disease, treatment involves intensive care with fluid therapy in a veterinary hospital or special clinic.

Prevention of illness is always preferable and vaccination is very effective (p. 17).

CANINE DISTEMPER VIRUS

This is one of the oldest killer viruses. The virus is related to human measles virus and it can produce long-lasting damage to the dog even after apparent recovery. Breathing in and licking up the virus are the routes for infection to become established. Puppies aged 6-12 weeks are most susceptible, as their immunity to disease that comes through their mother's milk is weaker at this stage (as the maternal antibody falls below a protective level).

Signs: The incubation time for the virus is six to nine days after meeting the infection. A temperature rise, with loss of appetite and a watery discharge from the eyes is commonly seen and a runny nose that might appear to be no worse than a 'cold' becomes, in the later second stage, mucoid and catarrhal and is far more injurious. Diarrhoea and vomiting may cause dehydration. Later on, a persistent cough develops. The eye and nose discharge turns to a greenish yellow colour and becomes crusty, sticking to the nose edges and to the eyelid corners.

JUVENILE CELLULITIS AND DISTEMPER

A condition occasionally found in puppies aged three weeks to six months was often called 'head-gland disease'. Developing suddenly in 48 hours, the head of the puppy swelled, the eyelids and the lips appeared swollen and then discharged pus. If not treated, scarring and permanent hair loss around the muzzle might result; sometimes the joints seemed painful as well. The signs suggested an immune-mediated complex. It was often impossible to culture bacteria from eye swabs, but the disorder responded to glucocorticoids – the vet would choose the most appropriate cortisone product based on his experience using a high dose twice daily. Australian researchers suggested it was an 'atypical immune distemper syndrome' and they thought it was sometimes found to develop 10-14 days after a live vaccine had been used.

After this stage, when the dog may seem to have "turned the corner" and to be improving, the most devastating signs appear as nerves are damaged. Encephalitis (brain inflammation) takes the form of dullness then fits (p. 96). A nervous twitch known as 'chorea' can develop that is so severe the dog cannot rest or sleep. Paralysis of the hind limbs is another possible complication or a staggering gait weakness known as 'paresis'. Even if the dog survives all these it is likely that the muscle jerking continues indefinitely where even the jaw muscles chatter out of control. See also p. 96.

HERPES VIRUS

The virus is more associated with cat disease and, of course, another type affects people. The dog type is related to some human viruses, known as a large envelope DNA virus, and can cause death in puppies as part of the so-called fading puppy syndrome. Herpes in adult dogs can cause small blisters on the penis or vagina and may be associated with excessive discharges from these organs. The virus can also occur as part of the kennel cough infection.

ENTERO VIRUSES

There are many viruses found in the gastro-intestinal tract and many are of unknown benefit to the dog and do no harm. The harmful enteritis or diarrhoea viruses include:

- Parvovirus
- Coronavirus,
- Rotavirus

Parvovirus

Parvovirus can affect dogs of any age but puppies, where the maternal immunity is just wearing off (at 6 to 20 weeks), are most likely to become ill.

Signs: A severe, bloody diarrhoea, collapse and high temperature may develop. Death ensues from fluids lost unless intensive nursing care can be made available. The growing cells of the body can be damaged by the virus and as the heart muscle is more susceptible than others, sudden deaths were a feature of parvovirus infection when the disease first appeared many years ago.

Coronavirus

This is another contagious intestinal infection mainly found in puppies, but the diarrhoea is milder than with parvovirus and not so long lasting. There is a small rise in body temperature but most of the ill effects are through the subsequent dehydration.

TREATMENT FOR ENTERO VIRUSES

Good nursing and cleaning up vomit and soiled bedding is

required. Fluids by mouth can be offered in small quantities once the vomiting has ceased, but intravenous fluid therapy may be needed to combat the shock of the fluid losses. Parvovirus can affect dogs of any age but it can survive in the environment for months or even years, so, with all these infections, disinfection is essential
Rotaviruses are found in enteritis diseases of young animals often in association with other disease organisms of the intestines.

A Cocker Spaniel puppy with Parvovirus receiving a blood transfusion.

RABIES
This is a very serious disease, fatal to dogs and equally dangerous to any human who has had a rabid dog bite them or even had rabid saliva on an open wound or in the eye.

Signs: The symptoms of rabies are those of a damaged brain (encephalitis).
- Changes in the dog's behaviour may be one of the first signs shown.
- Salivation – as the disease develops, the dog dribbles with the tongue held out of opened jaws. The face muscles may be in spasm, giving the mad dog appearance. This is the so-called 'furious' form where the dog runs and snaps at anything

that crosses his path.
- The disease may instead take the 'dumb' form when the jaws are paralysed. The dog cannot take water or swallow, and it staggers about, then eventually dies.

Treatment: There is no effective treatment; dogs suspected to have rabies are taken away and put into isolation kennels to observe for the development of symptoms. Vaccination of any dog likely to be exposed to infection is strongly advised (see p. 18).

The pet passport system is designed to stop any dogs entering the British Isles that could be incubating rabies virus. To obtain a passport the dog

must be given vaccine early enough to have a later blood test to prove the vaccine has 'taken' and gives a full protection.

OTHER DOG VIRUSES
Reovirus is one of the viruses involved in canine infectious bronchitis but is not a major disease producer. Canine parainfluenza virus may be found with canine distemper virus, canine adenovirus type 2, canine herpes virus and other viruses of the kennel cough syndrome (see p. 87).

Viral papillomatosis is the first virus described that causes cancer-type warts known as papillomas. These are non-fatal but in the mouth the warts can interfere with eating and may bleed. Warts on the skin are not so prolific and cause fewer problems unless they appear between the toes of the feet, when they can cause lameness. Most viral warts disappear after a matter of weeks but can be removed surgically either by freezing (cryosurgery) or cutting them out under anaesthesia. Papilloma in the bladder may be due to a virus; they also may be found in the rectum and cause straining and general discomfort to the dog. The straining may be confused with an obstruction from a 'stone'.

CANCERS AND TUMOURS

Chapter 12

It is not known what causes cancer in dogs. The rapid division of cells and the dog's inability to stop these 'overgrowths' is no better understood than in humans where research scientists the world over are working to find an answer. It is known that there are inherited factors and the genetic make-up of some breeds, such as Bernese Mountain Dogs, makes them more liable to die in middle age from cancer. The survey of dogs' lifespan made by the Kennel Club/ BSAVA Scientific Committee through the Animal Health Trust's epidemiologists, has given a clear indication that cancer was the cause of 27 per cent of all deaths (while old age was given as a cause for only 15 per cent of deaths). Other evidence from human studies is suggesting a strong hereditary factor in individuals' susceptibility to certain cancer

types. Dog breeders have to work from a small 'gene pool' in many of the less popular breeds, but as yet there is no evidence to show that crossbred dogs or mongrels have any less cancer than other, purebred dogs.

Malignant (cancerous) tumours can spread, seeding small tumours in the liver or lungs, anywhere there is a good blood supply. Spreading in this way is known as metastasis. Putting a name to a tumour is necessary to predict the biology of the growth and decide on the risk of malignancy and spread. Treatment is based on such biopsy tests that allow cells to be viewed under the microscope.

Carcinogens are cancer-producing substances that clearly play a part in certain types of cancer; bladder cancers caused by chemicals are now better understood. Some benign (harmless) tumours, such as skin

warts, as well as papillomas, are known to be virus caused and it is possible that some other infectious agent will eventually be found that causes other cancers.

MAST CELL TUMOURS, SKIN TUMOURS

Mast cell tumours are the most commonly diagnosed skin cancers of dogs, especially common in Boxers and Retrievers. Mast cell tumours compose about 20 per cent of all skin tumours found. These tumours are difficult to diagnose and treat because they copy other, more benign, skin lesions. Mast cells vary over a wide range from benign to the very malignant – where up to 95 per cent will metastasise to other sites in the body, such as the liver, lymph nodes and the spleen. Histology tests (cells examined under the microscope) are needed to grade the mast cell type.

There are other nasty skin

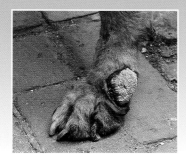

Skin tumour on the foot.

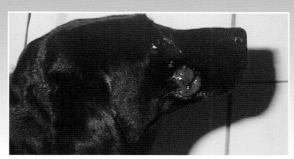

Squamous cell tumour on a Labrador's face.

tumours such as: squamous cell carcinoma, adenocarcinoma. Melanoma are the black-coloured skin growths. Many are benign, but in all cases of doubt, a biopsy of the cells should be taken so they can be examined under the microscope to determine their capacity to spread.

Lipomas or fat tumours only cause problems when they grow so large they press into the shoulder at the armpit or in the groin. As benign tumours there should be no difficulty in removing these and similar tumour types.

A squamous cell carcinoma is a tumour that starts off as a shallow skin ulcer but then invades the body. It needs immediate treatment, which involves surgical excision where possible, and possibly X-ray treatment to follow up. If the condition is not treated promptly, there is a risk that the cancer may spread to the lymph nodes and lungs.

Treatment: Excisional biopsies imply that the whole tumour is removed at one operation. Treatment by surgically cutting out (wide excision) the lump is very successful if diagnosed early enough with many tumour types. DNA vaccination for malignant melanoma represented a new breakthrough in cancer treatments and it represents one of many 'novel' treatments being developed for dogs with cancer.

MAMMARY GLAND TUMOURS

Mammary tumours are the commonest cancer of female dogs (skin tumours are the most common form of cancer in both males and females). They are quite common in older bitches, about half are benign and the other half malignant. Bitches spayed before or just after their second heat are very unlikely to develop mammary growths. This suggests that repeated heats and subsequent false pregnancies may have a strong influence on whether a tumour will form later in life.

Tumours can occur in one mammary gland or several of them. Malignant tumours spread their cells to an adjacent gland or through the lymph draining to the nearest lymph node – often the one in the inguinal region (inside the back leg). In the case of the front glands of the bitch being involved, spread can be through the axillary lymph glands in the armpit. Secondary tumours may then be found on X-ray in the lungs, following spread by either route.

Treatment: Removal at the first sign of a 'lump' by surgery is always advised and a biopsy will indicate the degree of malignancy present. Hormonal therapy, similar to that used after breast cancer in women after surgery, may be advised, but there are currently no regular treatments proved of benefit in dogs

LEUKAEMIA AND LYMPHOSARCOMA

The term leukaemia indicates that there are cells circulating in the blood stream coming from blood-forming tissue. These cancers usually involve the bone marrow, which forms blood cells (haemopoietic), or the lymph nodes, and in those organs that

PART II

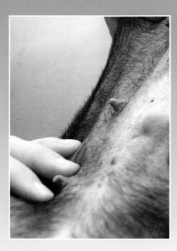

A mammary tumour.

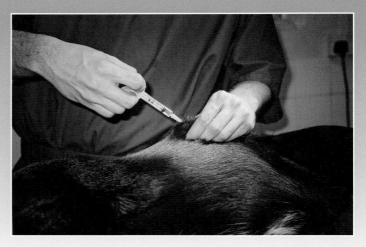

Lipoma tumour on a dog's back. A fine needle is being used to aspirate a sample, which allows the cells to be examined in the laboratory.

contain lymphoid tissue, such as liver and spleen. Leukaemias may take one of three forms: lymphoma cell leukaemia, acute leukaemia and chronic leukaemia.

These diseases may occur in dogs aged between six and nine years old especially the chronic form.

Signs: In the dog there are a variety of symptoms of vague ill health, and blood samples will be necessary to look at the red and white blood cells. Any lumps in the groin, armpit, chest or neck region may be lymphosarcoma and require veterinary examination; biopsy samples may be taken to help diagnosis. Chest and abdominal X-rays may be required too. Chronic leukaemias have a protracted clinical course and may only be

found when taking tests on dogs for other complaints. Skin ulcers may be present in cutaneous lymphosarcoma. It is rare but is one of the most unpleasant diseases, with ulcers in the skin that will not heal. In long-haired dogs the condition may not be recognised until it has spread so much that there is no effective treatment.

Leukaemia does not cause enlarged lymph nodes, but pale mucous membranes may indicate secondary anaemia and blood tests then taken may show leukaemic cells circulating in the blood. Other signs of this blood abnormality are body weakness, loss of appetite, bleeding from the gums at the margin with the tooth, and pinpoint bleeding spots may be found elsewhere. A further aid to diagnosis is a bone marrow biopsy.

Treatment: For many of these conditions anti-cancer drugs (chemotherapy) can be very effective. Even in advanced stages of the disease it may be put into remission (or halted) for months or years.

OSTEOSARCOMA
Bone tumours are found more often in the larger breeds of dog. Again there is a genetic predisposition to this sort of cancer. Dog breeds such as the Pyrenean Mountain Dog, Newfoundland, and St Bernard are 60 times more likely to develop this cancer than in the small breeds weighing less than 10kg. The rates for bone tumours in dogs are much higher than for humans. Any large dog that suddenly develops a limp in a front or back leg associated with a swollen, painful area of bone

should be sent for an X-ray or scanning, especially if there has been no recent injury.

Treatment: Early treatment with chemotherapy may be successful but a limb amputation may be the only resort to save a dog's life. Radiotherapy may be used to reduce bone pain as a form of palliative treatment.

Chondrosarcoma is a similar malignant bone tumour of the dog, but would be more likely to be found in a rib, the pelvic area or the nasal bones of the dog's face. Both sorts of tumour can spread to the lungs if not treated early enough to stop the spread.

OTHER CANCERS

Almost any part of the body may be affected with cancer. In many cases there will be neither growth nor a lump but the dog will show ill health. The skill of the veterinary surgeon is needed to find out the cause of the illness.

SPLEEN TUMOURS

Tumours of the spleen, known as haemangiosarcoma, have a high incidence in dogs. Spleen removal is the standard treatment but survival times are often short.

ANO-RECTAL TUMOURS

An adenocarcinoma is the most common growth in this area.

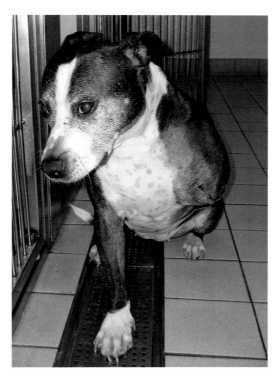

A Staffordshire Bull Terrier after amputation of the right fore leg. This was needed because a tumour was spreading up the leg.

Cancers in and around the anal sacs may be overlooked until bleeding occurs. Research into a breed disposition for this sort of growth is necessary following suggestions that Cocker Spaniels amongst others are more often affected.

REPRODUCTIVE CANCERS

Tumours may occur in the testicles of older dogs. Some types produce feminisation.

The ovaries, bladder or prostate are some of the many possibilities where cancer may attack the dog.

BRAIN TUMOURS

Brain tumours are quite rare but the Boxer breed is more affected than other older dogs. Early-stage diagnosis may be difficult, as symptoms are vague. Usually the vet will try to get a biopsy specimen for laboratory confirmation of a cancer. X-rays, ultrasound and blood tests may all help in finding the cause of such a problem. Chemotherapy is becoming more and more successful for many tumours, but certain breeds, such as Collies, are known to be at greater risk from toxicity.

TREATMENT FOR OTHER CANCERS

There is little that can be done to help in nursing such cancers in the home, but nutrition with a higher caloric density diet is advised. When radiotherapy or chemotherapy drugs have been used it is essential to follow any instructions given by the treatment centre. Some dog owners will ask a veterinary herbalist to make up a preparation with four or five different herbs that can support a dog who is undergoing chemotherapy and assist recovery.

Cancer can be treated, if not fully cured, in the same way that diabetic dogs are not 'cured' but regular medication preserves an active life for the dog.

PART II

DISORDERS OF NERVOUS ORIGIN

Chapter 13

When a dog is acting strangely or behaving out of character, the possibility of a neurological condition should be considered.

A dog that has suffered any severe head injury, such as after a road accident, will show clear signs of disruption of the central nervous system. If the brain is damaged, there may be coma or the dog may develop convulsions due to internal pressure on the brain from a skull fracture or internal bleeding. Further tests will be required to localise the pressure. Referral to a neurological centre for examination may give the best results.

INFECTIONS AFFECTING THE BRAIN

Although some nerve disorders are inherited or may be congenital, the brain and nerves can suffer with infectious diseases. Meningitis may be one possible cause of atypical behaviours. Fortunately, this inflammation of the surface membrane of the brain and spinal cord is rare in dogs. It can be caused by bacteria that reach the membranes (known as meninges) through a blood stream infection or after a deep penetrating wound near the spine. Middle ear infection or sinus infection can spread on to the brain surface. Treatment with antibiotics and a sampling of the fluid around the meninges can result in a rapid cure. Bacterial infection of the central nervous system is relatively rare and fever is only found in half the cases; the rest have normal body temperatures, so diagnosis often requires tests to be made. Toxoplasmosis and Neosporosis are examples of small protozoal organisms that cause nervous tissue damage as encephalomeningitis; muscles too are damaged with progressive hind leg paralysis. Blood samples and muscle biopsies are needed to diagnose the disease before treatment is given.

Canine distemper viral encephalomyelitis will develop two to three weeks after infection and sometimes there are none of the earlier signs affecting the respiratory and gastrointestinal systems (see p. 89). Encephalitis (inflammation of the brain) was seen more commonly when canine distemper virus affected many dogs. Signs did not develop at first with the virus infection but perhaps several weeks after the distemper illness was recognised. A dog would then develop a staggering gait, epileptic seizures, twitching (know as chorea) or a marked behaviour change. With the wider use of magnetic resonance

A Yorkshire Terrier suffering from epilepsy.

imaging (MRI) of the dog, it has become easier to make a diagnosis. Samples of the fluid round the brain (CSF) may be used to look for antibodies to distemper affecting the dog.

Treatment: The type of infection must be found first. Treatments with corticosteroids to reduce swelling in the brain is now less favoured, but other drugs can be used to reduce brain swelling; antibiotics for bacterial infection, and anticonvulsants when fits develop can all be used.

SEIZURES AND FITS

The first time a dog has a fit, people standing around cannot comprehend such a change in the dog's demeanour. The chomping and chewing suggests it might be epilepsy. The dog salivates from the mouth, kicks frantically and often voids faeces or urine in an uncontrolled manner, not recognising anyone. These signs are caused by an abnormal electrical activity spreading across the brain,

technically called an excessive discharge of hyperexcitable cortical neurones and it will probably only last a few minutes. Seizures lasting longer than five minutes could lead to more brain damage. Clusters of seizures over several days may be expected. Many dogs have only one fit each month: with this infrequency, medication may not be required.

Causes: The fit or seizure may be due to:
- An inherited weakness from one or both parents
- A head injury, such as a skull fracture after a road accident
- Brain tumour
- Some chemical disturbance in the blood stream (metabolic or toxins)
- Infection or inflammation.

Recent research on nervous disorders has shown that in some breeds, such as the Wirehaired Dachshund and the Basset Hound, a gene mutation is responsible for the condition known as Canine Lafora's disease. A quarter of these Dachshunds are thought to be carriers, although only five per cent will develop twitching and epilepsy between five to nine years of age. This gives hope that with more research, other hereditary causes of epilepsy may be able to be recognised, and such ill health can be eliminated by selective breeding.

A gene mutation in the Wirehaired Dachshund is the cause of Canine Lafora disease (progressive epileptic seizures induced by touch or excitement).

UNCONSCIOUSNESS AND COMA

The brain controls all of the nervous system. If there is an injury, such as a car accident, the pressure on the brain my cause loss of conscious sensations. The dog stares ahead and does not move his eyes since the nerve supply to the iris muscles comes from the mid brain, which may be under pressure from blood or fluid in the cranium. The condition of sub-dural haemorrhage fortunately is uncommon in dogs. As the cerebellum and mid brain become compressed, the breathing centre is also affected, so the breaths are deeper and less frequent.

A dog in a coma cannot feel pain and cannot be roused by shining lights or shouting. An unconscious dog may choke on its own vomit ,so it is best to open the mouth, pull the tongue as far forward as possible and look to see that there is nothing in the mouth.

Causes: There are many possible causes of coma:
- Heat stroke
- Hypothermia
- Low blood sugar
- Brain tumour
- Head injury
- Tetanus
- Poisons can cause deep sleep before death occurs

Treatment: First-aid treatment is to ensure a clear airway, wrap the dog in a blanket and convey him to the veterinary surgery. Obtain as much information as possible about accidents or other relevant history. Such patients may need nursing in a 24-hour critical care unit with expert nursing.

Treatment: Epilepsy in dogs needs careful selection of appropriate medication for treatment, and once commenced usually requires a life-long dosing, since a full cure is, at present, unlikely. The standard drugs used are phenobarbitone and the even more traditional bromide. The drug of choice for a fit often is diazepam, which can be obtained for home treatment by the use of a prepared syringe inserted into the dog's rectum. Some of the preparations used on people may have quite different results in dogs, but many of these have been tried when attempting to control the severely epileptic dog. The new group of drugs called 'AEDs' used for human epileptics are very effective and some have shown promising results in dogs where standard medication has not worked (which may be in as much as one in three dogs afflicted) with fits.

Herbal remedies may also be popular but should not be used as a replacement when conventional medication is effective at reducing the fits. The commonly used valerian root is a natural remedy, but there has been little scientific evidence to show it works and at higher doses could cause liver damage.

Milk thistle preparations can be given long term, and, in the case of a dog receiving phenobarbitone for fits, it may allow for a lower dose of the anticonvulsant to be used. However, your veterinary surgeon should be consulted before altering a dose regime.

SPINAL INJURIES

With any injury to the neck or spine the dog should not be moved unless he is stretched out on a board or a stretcher. Kinking the vertebral column, as when lifting a dog in the arms, may turn a simple injury into one with permanent paralysis.

PART II

NORMAL VERTEBRAE/SPINAL CORD   INTERVERTEBRAL DISC DISEASE

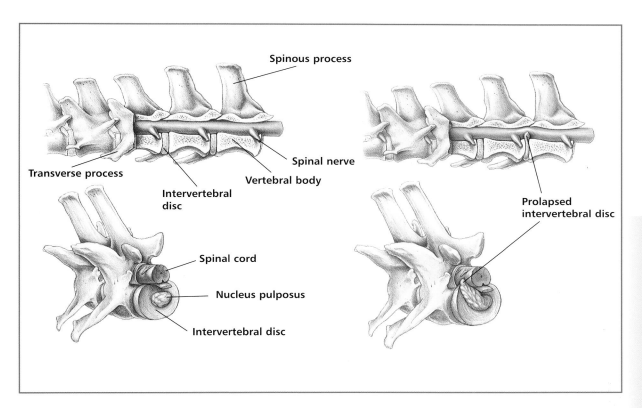

Spinous process

Transverse process

Spinal nerve

Vertebral body

Intervertebral disc

Spinal cord

Nucleus pulposus

Intervertebral disc

Prolapsed intervertebral disc

Causes:
- Intervertebral disc disease – the 'slipped disc'
- Fracture
- Tumour
- Fibrocartilagenous embolism
- Narrowing of the spine canal – the Wobbler syndrome.

These may be another manifestation of a disease that affects the nervous control between the brain and the extremities. The slipped disc is most often seen in longer-backed dogs. A fibrocartilagenous embolism produces the same sudden-onset paralysis but it is like a foreign body on the spinal cord. Large breeds, such as the Borzoi, Dobermann and Great Dane amongst others may suffer from instability of the neck vertebrae; the gait sways and dogs are known as 'Wobblers'. The disease may progress to paralysis.

Treatment: Operating to correct some of these conditions may be very successful. Recovery of the nerve supply to the legs may take months rather than weeks. Physiotherapy and massage under veterinary supervision will help recovery. Hydrotherapy (see p. 134) is particularly appropriate, as the buoyancy of the water helps to support the body as the legs paddle forward. A schedule of progressive therapy should be followed – not asking too much early on.

COLLAPSE
'Fainting' or intermittent collapse is more usual than sudden collapse followed by a loss of consciousness then death. Syncope (loss of consciousness caused by a fall in blood pressure) due to heart irregularities in breeds such as Boxers and Dobermanns, may be life threatening. Strokes are not

PART II

considered common in dogs but older dogs showing suggestive signs should always have their ears and heart examined by a vet. A stroke can be caused either by bleeding into the brain or from a blockage of the supply of blood due to an embolism or a thrombus.

The nature of a intermittent collapse is that it happens 'all of a sudden'. A dog that may have only seemed a bit slow suddenly collapses, cannot move or lies on his side paddling, and may appear unconscious. Syncope and fainting usually happen during exercise, while seizures have more predictable signs in a resting dog It is more likely that other causes lead to the dog collapsing and lying on his side.

Causes: Causes of collapse include:
- Cardiovascular diseases
- Severe shock, with the heart and lungs barely working
- Bone or spine disease
- Low blood sugar. Metabolic disease is seen in gundogs that collapse
- Any abdominal pain, or muscle spasms.

Treatment: In cases of collapse, once an airway is ensured, the

SYRINGOMYELIA DISEASE

This is a malformation of the hindbrain fluid system, with fluid-filled cavities found in the spinal cord of the upper neck. Mainly found in the King Charles Spaniel breed, MRI screening tests are used from an early age to look for these defects as they do not appear with X-rays. 'Fly catching' was the behaviour previously described for the behaviour of twisting the neck and looking up in the air for an imaginary fly. The disordered dog often showed a scratching of the shoulder region sometimes with painful screams when the head position was altered. Some affected dogs have a 'bunny hopping' gait. Treatment at present is not very effective and only alleviates the symptoms, but a neurologist's opinion may be advised.

dog may be left undisturbed for up to an hour to see if it revives, but is best taken to the vet for examination and diagnosis. Collapse as seen in working gundog requires an immediate source of carbohydrate (a sweetened oat bar).

Treatment for shock with fluids may be needed. Sometimes the vet may use corticosteroids for brain swelling and anticonvulsants to control fits. If there is an improvement in the first hours then a near full recovery may result with careful nursing.

METABOLIC NEUROLOGICAL DISEASE DUE TO L-2-HYDROXYGLUTARIC ACIDURIA

As a result of studies in America and the UK on the structure of the canine genome, it has been possible to pin-point a number of hereditary disorders by testing for a specific DNA defect. The ability to recognise the cause of unusual behaviour, ataxia (unsteady walking) and seizures (fits) became possible in 2001 in affected Staffordshire Bull Terriers and subsequently in one other breed (West Highland White Terriers). The test, now available by specialist laboratories (such as the Animal Health Trust in the UK, and Optigen, Health Gene and PennGen in the USA), can identify carrier dogs that are then considered unsuitable for breeding and can also be used to identify dogs already having the disease.

BEHAVIOURAL DISORDERS

If a dog becomes unusually aggressive, confused or disorientated, or barks without reason, these behavioural traits may be due to a disease of nervous origin or even pain. Many behavioural disorders are attributed to problems that develop in puppyhood, often produced by humans who have little or no idea of a dog's needs or how to train the dog. Young dogs should not be treated as 'little humans' and their responses to you are not those of a child. A dog being destructive in the home is probably under exercised and bored. Just because he chews at a treasured piece of furniture does not mean he is trying to 'pay you back' for some previous thing you have done with him.

Causes: Behaviour caused by a neurological state is seen in dogs that have:

- A skull fracture, received perhaps after a road traffic accident that was not witnessed by the owner. Recovering apparently fully from a wound on the head, months later the dog might show aggression or even epileptic convulsions.
- Brain tumours are not common but the first signs noticed will be a behaviour change and possibly later seizures. The dog with a brain tumour could show staggering when walking, nystagmus (the very rapid rocking of the eyes from side to side) and leg weakness or paralysis later as the pressure on the brain increases.

Diagnosis: Skull fractures will be

A head halter will give you better control, and will be accepted by the dog if it is linked with a reward.

seen after X-rays have been taken. The diagnosis of a brain tumour is made by a neurological examination and special tests including brain wave recording (EEG), cerebrospinal fluid analysis, CT scan or an MRI scan as necessary. This possibility should always be considered when a dog shows some unexpected behaviour change especially if middle-aged or older.

COPING WITH GENERAL BEHAVIOURAL PROBLEMS

First-aid for behavioural problems may be necessary. Separating fighting animals and the removal of things or situations that

provoke an 'attack' of the bad behaviour can be used in the short term. Everything should be done to avoid further confrontations until a referral with a behaviour consultant is possible.

Never commiserate with the fearful, anxious or aggressive animal. The bad behaviour may become reinforced by the words implying "OK" when in fact ignoring the dog or providing a distraction is the best method of disapproval. Saying in a weak voice "naughty" every time the dog lunges on the lead to attack a person or a well-behaved dog will not improve the situation. Don't gaze directly at the dog; turning the back away is less threatening. Providing an alternative activity that you can then praise repeatedly is the best way of trying to 'extinguish' such undesirable behaviour.

It can be useful to give the dog an opportunity to wear a muzzle or one of the various brands of 'head halters'. The owner should try to link the wearing of the item with a reward, such as first placing the muzzle or collar beside the food bowl at meal times. Rubbing the item on the dog's body as if stroking him allows the dog's body odour to permeate the material before use. Treats such as food rewards can be placed inside the head collar or muzzle. Before taking the dog out for a walk, place the muzzle on the dog a few minutes before leaving the house. The period of time the item is worn can be increased, and some dogs will even push their faces into the muzzle if they wish to anticipate the walk.

Referral to a behaviour consultant or counsellor can be an advantage for the long-term recovery of the dog's 'good' behaviour.

SOME SIGNS THAT WORRY DOG OWNERS

HEAD TILT

Most likely to be seen in the older dog, it is not always caused by a 'stroke', which is the first thing that comes to mind. The balance centre for the dog is contained in the inner ear, buried well in the bones of the skull. Otitis media (inflammation of the middle ear) can often spread into the inner ear, and the dog's balance centre becomes damaged. The dog holds his head as still as possible, may show pain by a tense facial expression, and avoids any interference, such as patting the head or trying to open the mouth. There can be a facial paralysis on the same side of the head with a drooping eyelid

PHEREMONES: A NEW WAY FORWARD

As a new method of helping the anxious dog: fear and pheremones go together. If a return visit is made to kennels for the rescue dog or even a routine visit to the vet's surgery, the dog's surroundings will lead to it showing anxiety. This may show as an initial growling, picking a fight with an adjacent dog or even getting in a quick bite before any other dog does it! A dog appeasing pheremone (DAP) has been used in waiting rooms for dogs (and their owners). Dogs exposed to DAP on their first visit to the vets were more relaxed and better behaved at later visits. See also Aromatherapy (p. 141).

condition known as Horner's syndrome.

A dog will carry his head slanting down on the painful side when the outer ear is infected. With this condition there is an obvious smelly discharge and redness and swelling of the skin folds around the ear.

Inner ear disease is sometimes called labyrinthitis, as the bony tubes or labyrinth contains the balance organ. Dizziness, loss of coordination and a staggered walk occur in severe cases. A dog may walk in small circles, lean towards the affected side, and

even the eyeballs may be seen to be affected with a rapid rocking movement, known as nystagmus. Vomiting may last for several days. Idiopathic vestibular disease is the name given to the disturbance of the peripheral vestibular system, and it will usually clear up itself and does not affect other cranial nerves. It is this sort that can be mistaken for a stroke since it develops quickly and then cures itself.

HEAD SHAKING

Ear mite infection was one of the most common causes of otitis externa, with head shaking and continuous scratching being the first signs. The mite is less common now as owners are more likely to have their pet's ears cleaned to remove mites and some of the more recently developed worm remedies also kill parasites in the ear.

Some dogs have ear allergies. Dogs with canine atopy (see also p. 123) and food hypersensitivity dermatosis may develop itchy inflamed ears. Even the medication applied to ears for an ongoing infection may produce a response, and those containing neomycin have been blamed for continuing the ear irritation. A grass seed in the ear canal produces violent head shaking and scratching. Foreign bodies are more common in dogs with hairy ears (such as Cocker Spaniels) in late summer as grass seeds ripen. If the condition is recognised immediately then the vet using an otoscope to illuminate the inside of the ear canal will be able to draw out the cause of irritation. The seeds have fierce points and barbs that mean the seed can only move forwards and such movement towards the ear drum is more likely as the dog scratches the ear with his foot. The ear responds by coating the seed in thick brown ear wax, but often the ear drum becomes punctured and loss of hearing will result. Many times a vet has treated a long-standing problem of a discharging ear with constant head shaking only to find a month-old (or older) grass seed well down inside the ear.

MOUTH SPASMS

When these occur the dog may look as though his mouth is fixed, with the teeth exposed as if the lips are in spasm.

Spasm of the mouth muscles may occur before or after a fi., The whole body may develop 'tonic-clonic' activity seen as twitching. Fortunately, a rare and unlikely situation, but it could be a sign of tetanus (also known as lockjaw) and urgent treatment is needed. At the present time in the UK an even more remote likelihood is the 'dumb' form of rabies where the throat and jaw muscles become fixed. As the dog is unable to swallow, drools of ropey saliva may hang from the mouth; the mouth is more likely to hang open. Coughing gagging and foaming will be present, which distinguishes these nervous signs from tetanus. Other nervous disease, such as distemper, can cause tightening up of the teeth and the exposure of the gums. A similar condition occurs in tetany and this was most commonly seen among bitches feeding puppies that developed eclampsia from a calcium shortage.

PART II

REPRODUCTIVE DISORDERS

Chapter 14

The bitch's reproductive system should function to ensure that the next generation of puppies can be produced so as to maintain the genetic line (the DNA). In order to maintain or improve the breed of dog, from fertilization of the egg to the moment of birth, functions occur at stages in the reproductive tract of the bitch. The male dog has a similar need to contribute half of the genes to the next generation and is suitably equipped to ensure fertilisation when the bitch is on heat. The overall control of the breeding cycles comes from each dog's brain, where the pituitary gland produces the controlling hormones.

Signals sent out by the bitch when she is ready for mating are shown by her behaviour and body posture; external chemical messages known as pheromones are also secreted. During the bitch's life she may come on heat (oestrus) perhaps 20 or 30 times; reproductive ability does not stop in middle-age, but the seasons may become less frequent and fertility will decline with advancing years.

The male remains fertile throughout his life and is still capable of siring puppies at 17 years old: the sperm count may be diminished, but a fertile bitch has been known to produce a healthy litter from such a mating.

Diseases of the reproductive system are more common in older dogs and bitches. There are positive health benefits from neutering females not intended for breeding at a young age – before their second season. Male dogs that develop prostate enlargement or anal adenoma in older age often will need castrating to control the diseases.

THE FEMALE

Irregular seasons in the entire (unneutered) bitch will be of concern if the dog owner wants to breed a litter of puppies (or if holidays or other absences are being planned). It is generally assumed that a bitch has a season or 'heat' every six months, but this pattern does not always follow. In the domestic canine, the period when there is no hormonal sexual activity, or anoestrus, lasts only about four months. Many wild carnivores breed only once a year, with their young being born at such a time when the greatest supply of food is available to ensure the mother's milk flow is stimulated, and later provide for solid nourishment at the time of weaning of the young. In some larger breeds of dog, this once-a-year pattern may be reverted to with little or no sign of a heat in the autumn or winter.

The optimum time for mating a

bitch on heat is not precise, but the average bitch ovulates at around 12 days, after the first sign of bleeding (pro-oestrus). Mating on the 12th and 14th days of a heat is customary: there is a fairly long time when the released eggs remain fertile in the fallopian tubes and spermatozoa can survive for some time after being deposited in the female reproductive tract, which allows a wider spread for good fertility.

When artificial insemination is used to produce pregnancy in 'difficult' bitches, or when used for other reasons, laboratory tests are available that pinpoint ovulation and the correct time to introduce the sperm – a 90 per cent success rate is claimed using such laboratory techniques.

CAUSES OF IRREGULARITY

- Split heats in the young bitch may be due to insufficient hormone output – a second heat starts 2-10 weeks after the first, rather short heat.
- Silent heats – the bitch has a normal cycle and may ovulate but shows no external signs of oestrus.
- Older females seem to come on heat less frequently and not at predictable times.
- The hormones that control oestrus are affected by nutritional status, daylight or disease: the heat may be delayed or there are no heats – known as anoestrus.
- Pyometra in the older bitch may produce discharges similar to oestrus (see below), confusing the observer.

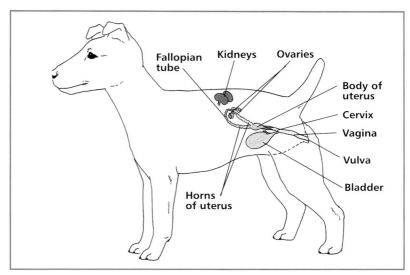

FEMALE REPRODUCTIVE SYSTEM

Cystic endometrial hyperplasia, commonly developing as a pyometra, is the most common uterine disease of the bitch. In young animals, the lining of the uterus quickly returns to normal after the heat is over. But in the middle-aged to older bitch, it is not uncommon for cysts to develop in the glandular lining of the uterus as reproductive hormones are secreted less actively. The warning signs are a bitch that becomes dull and depressed, and then later shows an unexpected, blood-tinged discharge. The more dangerous situation is the closed pyometra when there is no visible discharge. If infection produces pus within the uterus, toxaemia from the uterine contents leads to the bitch vomiting, often with frequent urination, and, in due course, septic shock. Pyometritis, as it is more correctly called, is

the result of hormonally induced changes occurring around 45 days after the end of the last heat. In all cases of pyometra, the course of action is to operate with an ovariohysterectomy, following the stabilisation of the ill dog with fluid therapy and with antibiotics. A recent development is the medical treatment of pyometra, which has a reasonable rate of success if there should be special reasons why the bitch is not neutered.

PREVENTION OF PYOMETRA

The routine neutering of all females, either when puppies or after the first heat, is advised as a safeguard measure except where it is intended to use a bitch for breeding. As well as stopping the uterus becoming diseased, there is an additional benefit in that cancer of the mammary glands is also prevented by spaying a bitch

Diseases of the reproductive system are more likely to affect the older dog.

OTHER DISEASES OF THE FEMALE REPRODUCTIVE TRACT

Diseases of the ovary are rare. Ovarian cysts can occur, but as these arise from the fluid in the ovarian bursa, they do not produce hormones that might cause a persisting oestrous discharge.

Vaginitis is seen in young bitches before their first heat. Hormonal supplementation may be needed, but the condition usually resolves once the first heat has passed.

Causes: Infections such as herpes virus can be longer lasting in the young female. Outside the UK, the bacteria *Brucella canis* can be the cause of vaginitis and infertility. Routine swabbing of bitches before mating usually will only show normal 'commensal' bacteria to be present, but there was a fashion for giving a single dose of an appropriate antibiotic just before mating to reduce the bacteria count in the vagina and cervix. Male dogs are sometimes attracted to bitches with vaginitis, and can give the impression that the bitch is on heat due to their undue attention. Excessive licking of the bitch in the area of the vulva may also be an indication that vaginitis is present and that veterinary attention is needed.

Vaginal hyperplasia – any swelling or the prolapse of pink vulval tissue that bulges out of the lips of the vulva – is alarming. A prolapse of the uterus is extremely rare in the bitch, but a

before her second heat. This observation was based on research undertaken in the Guide Dogs for the Blind (GDBA) organisation in the UK. It is very, very rare for a spayed guide dog to develop a mammary tumour, and this has been observed in pet animals as well. Spayed bitches probably live longer and have less stress than bitches left to come on heat twice every year.

Complications that can affect the bitch following an ovariohysterectomy are few, but urinary incontinence (see p. 67) is one that can be distressing. Some breeds with pelvic 'profiles' (where the bladder is more contained by the pelvis) seem more likely to be affected than the other breeds where it is possible for the bladder to hang down into the abdomen, over the edge of the pelvic bone brim.

pink 'tongue' of vagina wall appearing through the vulva creates alarm. Constant licking and frequent urination may accompany the protrusion.

A vaginal tumour can appear as a long-necked polyp at, or just outside, the vulva. This is most likely to be seen during pro-oestrus, or in oestrus when vaginal ligaments are slackened. The polyp may have been present for months before it is first seen. Surgical removal is a fairly simple operation, but if left untreated the mass ulcerates and infection develops.

Causes: When the external genitalia appear swollen, the vulva in bitches is responding to hormones in the bloodstream. The most likely cause is the production of hormone for the onset of heat; it will be accompanied by an unusual attention to cleanliness with the bitch licking the perineal area. Infection can be introduced at this time, but bacteria normally live in the vagina without causing diseases (similar to bacteria in the mouth or other cavities).

In the spayed bitch, swelling is an abnormality and may indicate some oestrogen activity from the adrenal glands, or, very rarely,

PYOMETRA

Uterine horns
Body of the uterus
Cervix
Vagina
The tissue is friable and easily torn

Hill's Atlas of Veterinary Clinical Anatomy

(inset depicts normal anatomy)

from an ovarian fragment (unfortunately left within by the surgeon) that has become active in producing oestrogens some months after spaying. There are also free oestrogens in the environment and this may help to trigger a vulva swelling.

FALSE PREGNANCY

Although not part of the reproductive tract, the milk glands are controlled by the same hormones of pregnancy – the milk-forming hormone prolactin enters the bloodstream at the time that less progesterone is secreted.

The condition of false pregnancy will occur about six to eight weeks after the last signs of heat, being quicker than for the 63 days of a pregnancy. The

condition should not be the confused with a normal pregnancy, even though there may be abdominal enlargement, since the mammary glands develop only just before birth and fill with milk after the pups are born.

Signs:

- Milk can be expressed from the teats. Mammary gland swelling and loss of appetite might suggest some illness. False pregnancy is considered normal for an unneutered bitch.

- A bitch with swollen milk glands may also show many of the behaviour signs that would show before the birth of actual puppies.

- Nest making, withdrawing from human company, and attachment to small toys or other inanimate objects can be anticipated.

- Rarely, aggression can show as part of the hormone imbalance. Nursing inanimate objects (such as a soft toy) may occur. One dark-coloured terrier became attached to knobs of coal in a fireside bucket, and when her owner went to stoke the coals of an open fire in the grate, the bitch bit the hand of the lady who was wielding the poker!

PART II

MALE REPRODUCTIVE SYSTEM

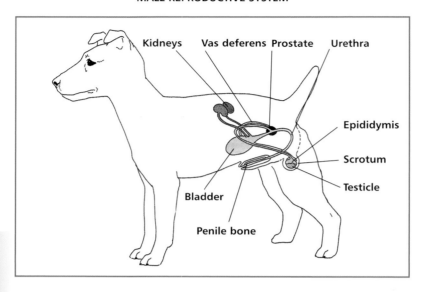

Kidneys · Vas deferens · Prostate · Urethra · Epididymis · Scrotum · Testicle · Bladder · Penile bone

a 10-day course or up to 16 days using a third lower dose rate.

THE MALE

The testicles actively produce testosterone hormone as well as functioning for producing and storing the sperm. Any excessive sexual activity on the part of the dog may be considered antisocial by humans who are not prepared for this form of 'play'.

UNDESIRABLE BEHAVIOUR

Young males undergo surges of hormone production in the run up to adulthood, and testosterone is largely considered to be the cause of urine-marking behaviour and young dogs mounting or riding other males or some non-canine objects. Antisocial sexual activity can be an embarrassment, especially since visitors and some people with stimulating odours trigger off displays of licking of the dog's swollen penis and 'humping' any available leg or soft object. Young puppies at 12 weeks practise riding on other puppies, then perform copulatory movements on feet or soft toys. Bare toes and even shoelaces excite the curiosity of puppies of both sexes.

Other antisocial activities can also be a problem: urine-marking objects outside the house can lead to the male puppy within the home lifting his back leg and marking curtains and other objects. This is all to do with establishing a dog's territory by putting down olfactory 'markers'. The objectionable behaviour can

Causes: The bitch, and some other wild carnivores, are under the influence of the hormone prolactin after the corpus luteum (producing progesterone) has remained active in the ovary for about 55 days. Prolactin is probably the principal hormone in female reproduction. The false pregnancy phenomenon may have developed as a canine group response when the hunting mother was absent from her cubs and unable to be present for suckling, or when unfortunately she might have been killed. The other females could act as 'aunts', nurturing and even feeding the puppies in the absence of the mother. This too would be useful when there is only one breeding cycle a year and all females ovulate at about the same time, though not all achieving a pregnancy. Prolactin affects the social behaviour of

wolf packs: with reduced prolactin output there is less aggression between females. Prolactin also has an effect on male wolves, with a smaller prostate and less sperm being produced.

Treatment: Potent anti-prolactin drugs (Cabergoline) can be used in the management of false pregnancy as a tablet given over four to six days. The same drug has been used for as long as 10 days to try to overcome aggression associated with false pregnancy, and with elevated prolactin levels in spayed bitches. Progesterone medication formerly used in false pregnancy is now less favoured. Bromocriptine is another very effective drug for false pregnancy; it inhibits the release of prolactin from the pituitary gland of the brain. Tablets can be given twice-daily as

PART II

A male Jack Russell Terrier being given an intravenous injection for general anaesthesia prior to being castrated.

A male's testicles should be checked regularly for signs of soreness or enlargement.

be discouraged by more exercise opportunities well away from the home, verbal chastisement if the puppy is caught in the act of marking, or applying appropriate deterrent smell applications.

It may be considered that 'roaming' or wandering away from the home by normally well-behaved dogs is a sign of abnormal sexual activity, but this is a characteristic response to the scent of a bitch on heat. In one dog this involved a journey of three miles to the next Oxfordshire village where the only unspayed bitch in the locality resided! A dog that is concerned about the smell of a bitch may stop eating and try to escape from the house if the door is very slightly ajar. Male dog problems may be avoided or treated by the removal of testicles, i.e. castration, but this can be inappropriate if only a

minor problem is observed.

For the treatment of hypersexuality, an injection of Delmadinone reduces the level of aggression because it has a central calming effect. Treatment should be repeated after eight days if there is no response. Animal behaviourists often advise castration when aggression is shown by a dog, but it is only an ingredient in the treatment of the whole aggression problem. In situations of fear or anxiety-related aggressive behaviour, surgical removal of the testicles can exacerbate the behaviour. There is also available a contraceptive implant for dogs that causes temporary desexing for six months.

DISEASES OF THE MALE REPRODUCTIVE SYSTEM

Cryptorchidism means hidden testicles. Nearly all breeds carry

a recessive genetic factor – the absence of one or both testicles is due to their retention in the abdomen or inguinal (groin) region. At first it will only cause infertility, but there is a greater risk of tumours when the testicle remains inside the abdomen than when made cooler by lying in the scrotum away from the abdomen.

Orchitis is the inflammation of one or both testicles. It is rare, but occurs after trauma as in a road accident. *Brucella canis* bacterial infection has to be considered, but is not a problem in the UK at present.

Tumours of the testicles are seen quite frequently in middle-aged and older dogs. The obvious signs of a swelling may not be noticed at first, but the production of excess hormones, sometimes female ones, causes behaviour such as

PART II

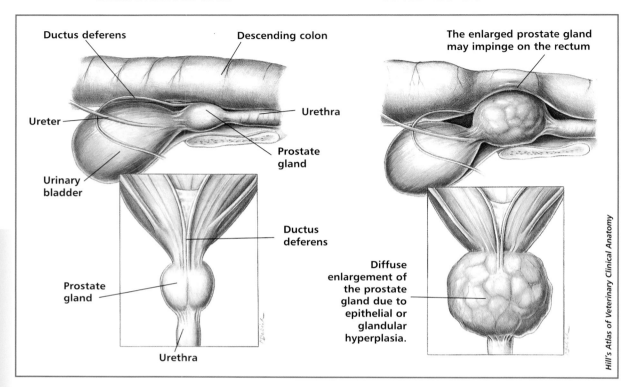

NORMAL PROSTATE GLAND

Ductus deferens
Descending colon
Ureter
Urethra
Urinary bladder
Prostate gland
Ductus deferens
Prostate gland
Urethra

BENIGN PROSTATIC HYPERPLASIA

The enlarged prostate gland may impinge on the rectum

Diffuse enlargement of the prostate gland due to epithelial or glandular hyperplasia.

Hill's Atlas of Veterinary Clinical Anatomy

attraction by other male dogs.

Prostate disease of older dogs cause difficulty in urination, but, more often, there is straining as if the dog is constipated (due to the enlarged prostate gland pressing upwards into the rectum).

Treatment: In many of the testicle disorders, castration is an easily applied remedy. Treatment of prostate disease may require antibiotics if infection is present, or anti-male hormones are used. The surgical drainage of a prostate abscess might be required, but it is extremely rare that the removal of the prostate gland is advised.

Also available is a long-acting anti-androgen, which acts on the prostate but maintains normal reproductive function; it can be used for benign enlargement of the prostate gland in dogs. The seven-day tablet treatment provides rapid benefits and lasts six months before more treatment is needed.

LAMENESS AND JOINT PROBLEMS

Movement in the dog involves all four legs working together, taking the weight evenly. Any injury or disorder of the muscles, nerves, bones, ligaments, tendons or the joints may result in limping or more severe signs of disease.

LAMENESS AND JOINT PROBLEMS

Most joint problems may be recognised when the dog seems stiff when getting up, or, after a walk, seems to be 'favouring' or taking less weight on one leg than the other three. Many joint diseases only develop gradually and are possibly not seen until a dog is five years old or more. The lameness then often improves as the dog moves about or when exercised. If the joint is bent by hand, a creaking known as crepitus may be felt, suggesting the joint is no longer lined by smooth cartilage or there may be new bone forming around the rim of the joint. Long walks on hard pavements may make other types of joint disease worse; inflammatory arthritis has joint pain and a raised temperature as a sign.

Some lameness is more associated with injury of the younger dog, such as cruciate ligament rupture or a hereditary weakness causing patellar luxation. There are also hereditary factors to consider in joint diseases, such as hip and elbow dysplasia (osteochondritis dissecans, see p. 114). Schemes to screen parents of future litters by X-rays have gone part of the way to reducing the severity of such conditions, allowing dogs to live longer without chronic pain. When many joints are swollen or painful, this might suggest a situation similar to human rheumatoid arthritis, known as immune-mediated arthritis.

DEGENERATIVE JOINT DISEASE

The healthy joint is lined with soft cartilage with a film of lubricating fluid commonly known as 'joint oil'. Heavyweight dogs are more likely to show symptoms earlier as the cartilage wears thin and the lubrication becomes less. With time the joint suffers more wear and tear, developing the type of arthritis known as osteoarthritis.

Treatment: There are many effective treatments for joint pain, but it is suggested that a veterinary examination to 'work up' the cause of lameness is advisable before treatment is commenced. X-rays, bone scans, computer tomography and analysis of the joint fluid (synovial fluid analysis) may all

FORELIMB SKELETON

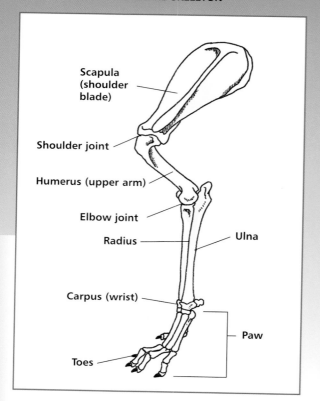

Scapula (shoulder blade)

Shoulder joint

Humerus (upper arm)

Elbow joint

Radius

Ulna

Carpus (wrist)

Paw

Toes

HINDLIMB SKELETON

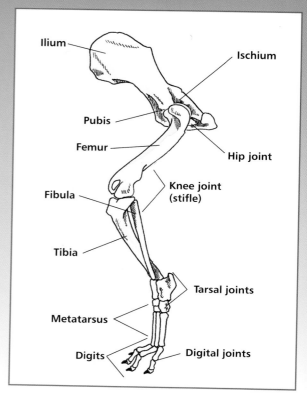

Ilium

Ischium

Pubis

Femur

Hip joint

Fibula

Knee joint (stifle)

Tibia

Tarsal joints

Metatarsus

Digits

Digital joints

be called for. The simple remedies at home are to allow a dog to lie at full length rather than curled up in a smaller basket, so the dog can find his most comfortable resting position. Obvious factors, such as cold stone floors and draughty places, should be avoided. Of the home remedies, aspirin is probably the safest, but human medication should be avoided, as the liver of the dog metabolises some of the more advanced arthritis remedies in a way that could produce toxicity. Aspirin can be given at a low dose of 10 to 20 mgm per kilogram of bodyweight of the dog, repeated every 12 hours (it is now well recognised that the same dose for a cat would be poisonous). The smaller breeds of dog will require minute doses compared with the body mass of a human under medication. When inappropriate medication is used, fatal results may be anticipated, with gastric haemorrhages, liver and kidney failure. Therefore, always consult a vet before beginning any treatment at home.

A safer herbalistic approach for arthritis, whether chronic or acute, is to use an extract of dandelion leaf (*Taraxacun officinalis*) especially for the sort of stiffness that gets worse in the winter or spring; sensitive joints may respond to the changes in barometric pressure, noticeable most when the air becomes damper.

JOINT INJURIES

Limping may be seen as the dog walks. It may only be slight as the dog first sets out for a walk, or it may be seen after a longer walk, becoming worse especially when a hard surface (such as a pavement or road) is used towards the end of the exercise period.

Trying to find the affected part of the leg may not be easy.

Recognition may be easier if the dog holds the leg up after licking at it and invites you to look at it. Where there is a shortening of the stride or a slightly uneven gait, it may be very difficult to identify the affected joint or muscle mass.

- It should be easy to find the protruding end of a thorn or shard of glass in the pad of the dog once the feet are washed.
- Sprains and strains occur after vigorous exercise, often over a rough field surface. The dog may be unable to bear weight on the leg. If this is still the case after 24 hours, veterinary attention is required.
- Tearing of the cruciate ligaments of the knee joint. Known as cruciate disease, this has become a more common problem in adult, heavier dogs (see p. 114). A sudden lameness after a jumping injury suggests that the rotation or overextension of the hind leg has resulted in a torn or ruptured ligament. Surgical repair is usually then necessary in order to avoid osteoarthritic changes later.
- Injury to the kneecap (or patella) may dislodge it from the groove in the front of the knee joint, known as patellar luxation (see p. 115). Mild cases can be controlled with regular exercise. Surgical repair may be needed. Some Jack Russell Terriers regularly run on three legs, hitching up if the patella luxates – and in no way does it slow their progress!
- Fractures and dislocations may

TYPICAL JOINT CONSTRUCTION

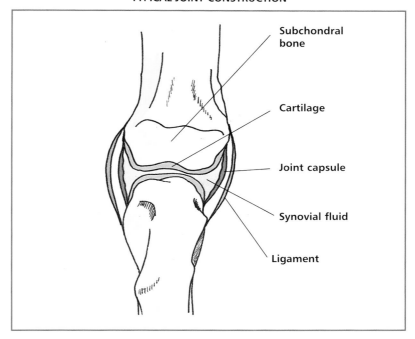

Subchondral bone

Cartilage

Joint capsule

Synovial fluid

Ligament

not be immediately obvious, but the sooner these are treated in the surgery, the better.

- Septic arthritis, known as Lyme disease, is common in the USA and occurs from time to time in the UK. Although it is an infection from tick bites, the sudden lameness often suggests a broken leg. Any dog bite wound or other penetrating injury may set up bacterial arthritis (see p. 85).

Treatment: Once the cause has been identified, consulting the vet is the best way of deciding whether medication and rest is required or some surgical operation. For first-aid, cold packs applied to an injured leg might consist of a pack of peas brought out of the deep freezer and held against a joint for 20 minutes. Wrap the leg in a towel to cover most of the leg and stay close by to reassure the dog. The dose of aspirin advised in the previous section may be helpful in reducing some of the destructive inflammatory responses.

Lyme disease requires antibiotics, as would any other injury where the joint is infected. Rickettsial arthritis from ticks is the cause of Rocky Mountain spotted fever and canine ehrlichosis: all forms of infectious arthritis need immediate specific veterinary treatment. Tick control/anti-tick preparations will be needed on a regular basis with such conditions.

PART II

PART II

OSTEOCHONDRITIS DISSECANS

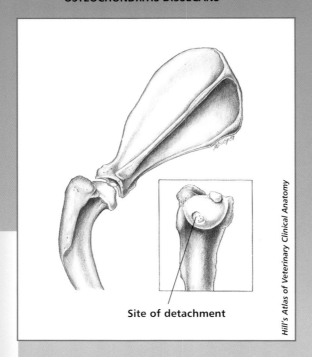

Site of detachment

Hill's Atlas of Veterinary Clinical Anatomy

SHOULDER JOINT

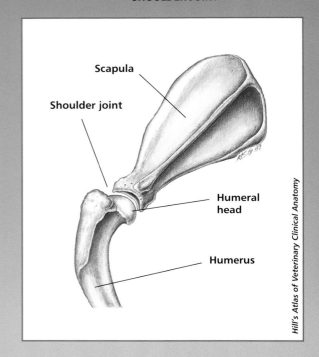

Scapula

Shoulder joint

Humeral head

Humerus

Hill's Atlas of Veterinary Clinical Anatomy

CRUCIATE LIGAMENT

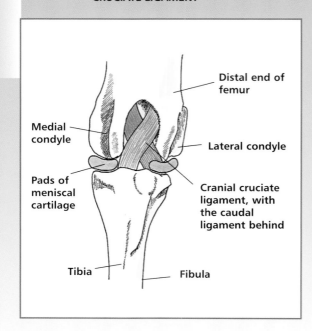

Distal end of femur

Medial condyle

Lateral condyle

Pads of meniscal cartilage

Cranial cruciate ligament, with the caudal ligament behind

Tibia

Fibula

RUPTURED CRUCIATE LIGAMENT

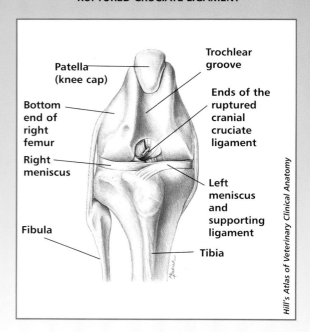

Patella (knee cap)

Trochlear groove

Bottom end of right femur

Ends of the ruptured cranial cruciate ligament

Right meniscus

Left meniscus and supporting ligament

Fibula

Tibia

Hill's Atlas of Veterinary Clinical Anatomy

PATELLAR LUXATION

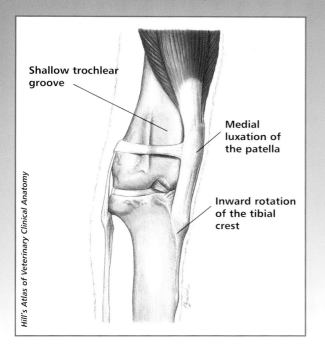

Shallow trochlear groove

Medial luxation of the patella

Inward rotation of the tibial crest

Hill's Atlas of Veterinary Clinical Anatomy

HIP DYSPLASIA

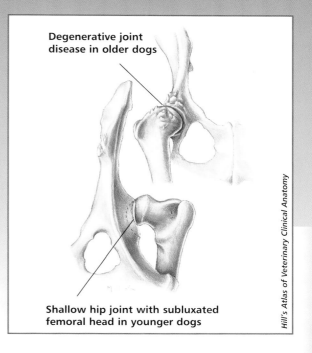

Degenerative joint disease in older dogs

Shallow hip joint with subluxated femoral head in younger dogs

Hill's Atlas of Veterinary Clinical Anatomy

PART II

INHERITED BONE & JOINT CONDITIONS

HIP DYSPLASIA

Dogs that inherit this disease can be identified by X-raying at 12 months of age (in the UK; other countries may have different ages to X-ray). There are many genes involved and environmental factors will decide how severely the dog will show lameness. The hip is a ball-and-socket joint, and if the cup is too shallow or loose, instability results with resulting signs of joint disease.

ELBOW DYSPLASIA

Known as osteochonritis

dissecans (p. 114), this can be identified in a similar control scheme, with X-rays that grade the joint on a 0-3 scale – the higher number being the worst. The disease takes several forms depending on which bones of the elbow joint are malformed.

More difficult to diagnose is the dog that has both hip and elbow dysplasia at the same time. An affected dog may show an uneven rolling gait, but a clue may be that when the dog stands still, the front toes are turned in and the elbows are bowed out slightly to relieve a dull ache in the elbow joints. If the hips are more severely affected, this can

be seen as the dog hoists himself up into a standing position. This will require some effort, and the dog may have a drawn expression on his face, particularly if he has rested for 20 minutes or more after a long walk.

Dogs seldom wince or cry out with pain, unless you touch the joint unexpectedly and the dog has no time to guard himself except by a whimper or a sharp cry. If you want to examine the dog, gently bend and flex a leg, extend all the toes in turn, then move up the leg, bending each joint in turn, in order to detect resistance or a pain response.

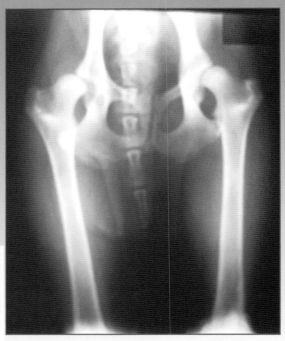

X-ray showing hip dysplasia in a six-month-old Collie.

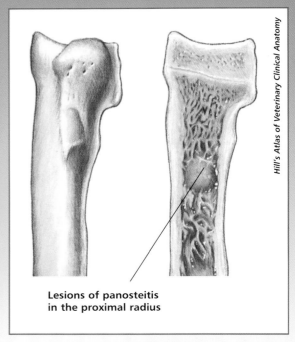

Hill's Atlas of Veterinary Clinical Anatomy

Lesions of panosteitis
in the proximal radius

PANOSTEITIS

PANOSTEITIS

This can be a cause of sharp pain when the bone is squeezed near a joint; it is sometimes called 'wandering lameness'. It is more likely to be seen in the young to maturing dog, and can also be a confusing factor when diagnosing elbow and hip joint pain. Males with more rapid bone growth are more affected than females and, with luck, the problem disappears soon after the dog reaches his first birthday.

WOBBLER SYNDROME

Seen in large breeds of dog, such as the Great Dane or the Dobermann, this is caused by compression of the spinal cord in the neck. There are often malformations of the neck bones, or cervical vertebrae, which leads to unequal pressure being put on the spinal cord that connects the brain's locomotor centre to the legs. It is of interest that these larger breeds, which have rapid bone growth, may also be the breeds where choke chains are most commonly used. Using a head collar, such as the Halti, is much safer in preventing neck injuries.

EQUINE CAUDA

A similar problem to Wobbler syndrome, this can occur in the lower back region, an area of the nerves known as the horse's tail or cauda equine. If there is compression of the spine at the level of the pelvis, early signs include pain, difficulty in getting up, and a recurring lameness on one or both back legs; a further problem can be loss of bladder and anal sphincter control. Testing for sensitivity in the lumbosacral region reveals increased sensitivity. The condition should be discussed with the vet, who will describe possible treatments to alleviate the condition.

INTERVERTEBRAL DISC DISEASE

This can take one of two forms: the sudden explosion of the soft

MUSCLE DISORDERS

Muscle disease is fairly rare in the dog; It might be seen as muscle weakness, wasting of the muscle mass, and lameness. Muscle strains can happen in athletic dogs. Tearing or stretching of the fibres that make up the muscle mass will be painful. The lameness that develops may persist for several weeks; the muscle affected may be tender when handled and may swell if bruised (although with a thick-coated dog any bruising is easily missed).

Causes:
- Immune-mediated myositis and megaoesphagus.

- Inherited weakness, such as 'floppy Labrador' (Labrador Retriever myopathy), seen as muscle stiffness. Difficulty in raising the head and dilation of the oesophagus may result.
- Endocrine disorders (e.g. hyperadrenocorticism, hypothyroidism, see p. 126).
- Infections, such as *Toxoplasma gondii*, *Neospora caninum*

Treatment: Once the condition has been recognised and a diagnosis made (which may involve blood tests and muscle biopsy), treatment will be provided by the vet specific to the condition.

contents of the disc cuts into the spine and causes an almost immediate hind leg paralysis. Less easily recognised is the other, slower bulging of the disc. This produces varying amounts of hind-leg foot dragging, paresis or pain in the back region. In long-backed dogs, such as Dachshunds, pressure on the spinal cord can occur further forward, just behind the last rib. It should be mentioned that, in the neck, bones might also allow disc contents to press on the nerves in the neck, causing pain and more widespread changes similar to those of Wobbler syndrome.

Treatment: Once the condition has been diagnosed, the vet will advise the best course of treatment. There are very effective anti-inflammatory drugs now available, so recourse to surgery is less frequent. Reducing the bodyweight of the dog always takes the strain off joints. As with all hereditary disorders, breeding from affected animals is discouraged.

PART II

SKIN DISORDERS

Chapter 16

The dog's skin may be subject to all sorts of injuries, and, as the largest organ of the body, it has many functions as well as protecting underlying structures.

SCRATCHING

Dry skin is often associated with those dogs living in a household environment and certain dietary factors have also produced a number of skin problems. Scratching on its own is not a disease, since some dogs will scratch when just bored. When faced with some mental dilemma, a dog may sit and scratch (displacement activity helps relieve the dilemma), and, as such, mild scratching can be considered a normal behavioural response. It can be compared with a car driver self-grooming the back of his or her neck after overtaking badly or completing a slightly hazardous manoeuvre – often while being observed in your rear-view mirror!

Things that cause a dog to scratch are multiple. It is necessary to consider the various parasites that can live on, or under, the dog's skin, as these may not be obvious but can be the cause of hair loss and persistent irritation. There are then other systemic diseases that involve dry skin and scratching tendencies.

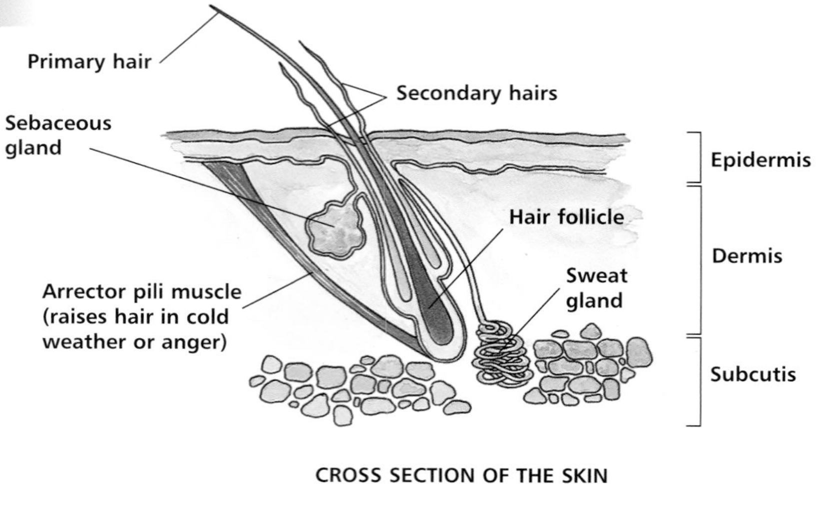

Primary hair

Secondary hairs

Sebaceous gland

Epidermis

Hair follicle

Dermis

Arrector pili muscle (raises hair in cold weather or anger)

Sweat gland

Subcutis

CROSS SECTION OF THE SKIN

FLEA HYPERSENSITIVITY

Flea biology and control has been the subject for extensive study, and there are now very effective methods of keeping this parasite away from the dog. A few flea bites in the young dog may set up an excessive immune response and the dog becomes overreactive (or hypersensitive) to contact with fleas for the rest of his life. Cats are now the main source of fleas affecting dogs. It is reported that each female flea can lay an average of 25 eggs a day and egg production will continue over 100 days. The hatching of these eggs is away from the dog and strongly influenced by environmental conditions; the most favourable conditions being warmth at 25C and a high relative humidity of 50 per cent. The problem of fleas is dealt with in Chapter Three. Fleas must be controlled and the veterinarian will discuss various ways in which hypersensitivity may be reduced.

MANGE MITES

These cause skin disease less frequently, as better hygiene and feeding help to promote resistance to chronic mange.

SARCOPTES LIFESTYLE

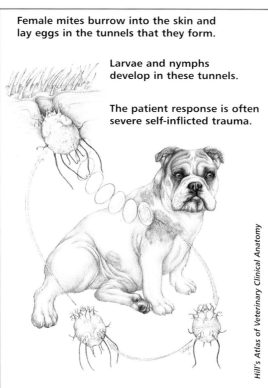

Female mites burrow into the skin and lay eggs in the tunnels that they form.

Larvae and nymphs develop in these tunnels.

The patient response is often severe self-inflicted trauma.

Hill's Atlas of Veterinary Clinical Anatomy

SARCOPTIC MANGE

Sarcoptic mange is spread by direct contact, so the dog may arrive home with intense scratching due to a parasite from another dog, even though there has been only a brief contact. The tendency for dogs to roll on organic waste matter can also be a cause. Mange mites are often associated with stray or neglected dogs; foxes and other animals may also be responsible for spreading mites.

Signs: The dog with sarcoptic mange will be very itchy. The ear tips and the face are affected.

Later, large areas of the legs or the flanks become hairless, scaly and red.

Treatment: The veterinary surgeon should be consulted about any severe scratching. Tests such as skin scrapings for a microscopic examination may be needed, and even then the mites may not be found on the first visit to the vet. Bath the dog with suitable mange preparations as advised; it will clear the skin, but repeat treatments may be required to prevent reinfection. The product selamectin, used as a monthly spot-on, is also effective against sarcoptic mange, used as three applications at two-week intervals.

DEMODECTIC MANGE

The second most common mange is demodectic mange. The tiny Demodex mite is able to live in the skin without causing too much harm, but when disease or poor nutrition lowers the animal's immunity, the mite becomes a problem and all the hair will be lost. Thinning hair around the eyes, the lips and the corners of the mouth may be seen, and sometimes the feet are affected. It was noticed that, in some bitches in training as assistance dogs, bare areas below the ears developed at the first heat, but they usually self-cure in six to eight weeks.

PART II

Signs: This type of mange is more often seen in short-coated breeds, such as Bull Terriers and Dobermanns. Demodex can be found in scrapings taken from deep in the skin or in hair pluckings. Foot infections with the parasite are found in breeds like the Shar-Pei. It may be necessary to obtain skin biopsies from these areas, as the underlying cause and secondary infection may be needed to be treated at the same time.

The parasite lives in the depth of the hair follicle and is often difficult to find; the bald patches and hair loss may be the first sign that this sort of mange is present. There may be little scratching or itching and no recent contact with another dog. The parasite becomes embedded in the skin at, or just after, the birth of the puppy and may lie dormant until some stress effect makes it become active.

A more severe form, rarely seen now, is generalised demodectic mange when nearly all the body is affected and the hair follicles became plugged with mites and skin scales.

Treatment: There is a growing tendency not to use potent chemicals to try to kill off the

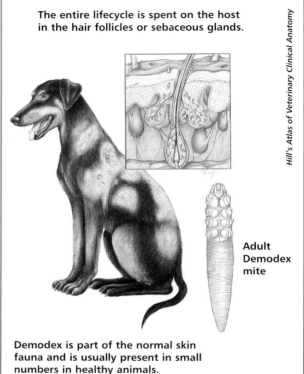

DEMODEX LIFECYCLE

The entire lifecycle is spent on the host in the hair follicles or sebaceous glands.

Hill's Atlas of Veterinary Clinical Anatomy

Adult Demodex mite

Demodex is part of the normal skin fauna and is usually present in small numbers in healthy animals.

parasite, but to improve the dog's immunity – only treating any secondary bacterial infections.

Both sorts of mange need veterinary advice, and experience will decide which medication is needed and for how long. Although this is such an old disease problem for dogs, there is only one drug licensed to treat canine demodeciosis in the UK and that is amitraz (Aludex, Intervet). A weak 0.05 per cent solution used as a dip is repeated every five to seven days until two negative skin scrapings or hair plucks are obtained. As a first

step, the dog's hair should be clipped very short. This is never popular, but after such treatment, flushing out the parasites from the hair follicles is much more effective when using a benzoyl peroxide shampoo.

Some other treatments are not licensed for use, and special permission will be needed by the vet from the owner. Heartworm treatments, which are available in many countries (such as tablets in the USA containing milbemycin), have been imported under special licence to the UK to treat resistant cases of demodectic mange.

EAR MITES

These are a special problem for dogs that have itchy ears. The parasite otodectes is usually caught from a cat. Close contact with the cat is not necessary, as a cat shaking its head can send the parasite in pieces of wax flying through the air and the mites land on the dog's coat.

Signs: One or two mites in the ear produce redness and intense irritation. If a dog scratches at his ear with his back toenails, scratch marks will be found on the ear, and bacteria can then infect this warm, moist, red ear area with severe consequences.

PART II

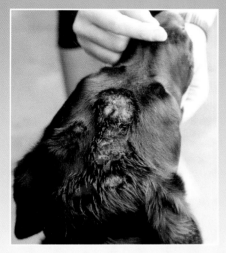

Head of a Labrador with furunculosis associated with ringworm infection.

Temperature and hours of daylight may have an effect on the coat.

Treatment: Treat daily for a week, using a suitable ear preparation: these are usually oil-based with an acaracide. Cats in contact must also be treated to reduce the risk of reinfection.

OTHER PARASITES

Lice, chiggers (Trombicula mites), walking dandruff (Cheyletiella mange) and ringworm are some other possible parasitic skin diseases diagnosed by the vet, who will also advise on the best treatment.

The most common parasite found in puppies with a white scurf or dandruff on their coats is Cheyletiella (pronounced key-let-e-ella). The puppy may not be itchy at first, but if you brush your hand against the lie of the hair on the back, more scurf comes off. Under the microscope, the eight-legged parasite looks like 'walking' dandruff. Hair is not lost from the puppy, but the coat on the back will be thinner; the parasite may also then walk on to humans and small, raised, itchy red spots appear on the person's arms or all over the body. The treatment for the human itching with the dog's Cheyletiella parasite is simple: as it feeds but does not live long, bathing or showering is sufficient to wash these mites away.

RINGWORM

This parasite causes hair loss, and humans can be infected by carrier animals. The cause is a fungus (not a worm), and the infection is spread by dead hair and scales or from direct contact with another animal. Cats should be considered as a possible source of the fungal infection, as they show few signs, but once a person is infected, an intensely itch skin condition can develop.

Signs: Scaly, very itchy spots are the first indications of ringworm; hairless areas may be later signs. Typical 'rings' on the abdomen are more likely due to a bacterial hypersensitivity response (see p. 124). Veterinary diagnosis is obviously of importance; there are good specific treatments for ringworm available as baths and tablets by mouth. Ultraviolet light is used as one test for ringworm hairs, known as a Wood's lamp, but it does not detect all ringworm varieties.

Treatment: The veterinary surgeon will decide which treatments are most appropriate. A skin wash may be prescribed for ringworm or a specific antibiotic for fungal infection; in

CHEYLETIELLA LIFECYCLE

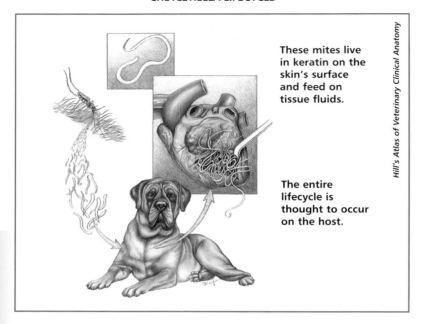

These mites live in keratin on the skin's surface and feed on tissue fluids.

The entire lifecycle is thought to occur on the host.

Hill's Atlas of Veterinary Clinical Anatomy

PART II

all cases, treatment may have to be prolonged. There will also be a warning that ringworm can be caught by people handling the dog, and good hygiene measures are necessary.

CHIGGERS

This is the name used for the harvest mite (Trombicula). This is now rare in the UK, but it was often seen in the autumn when dogs had walked through cornfield stubble after harvest. Affected dogs had very itchy feet; orange-brown mites could be found between the toes, but it was quite easy to wash them away with an anti-parasitic shampoo. If a parasite is causing hair loss on the paws, it may be easily killed with shampoos or Fipronil spray.

MALASEZZIA

This parasitic yeast is invisible to the eye. Found on normal skin, it can multiply in moist, inflamed skin; therefore, it is often found in large numbers in ear infections, and in atopic dogs or others with itching dermatitis. Specific treatments are available once the condition is diagnosed by microscopic examination. Shampoos containing chlorhexidine and miconazole are usually effective.

EXCESSIVE COAT SHEDDING

It is necessary for a dog to shed his summer coat before the winter so that a thick, denser coat can grow to protect against the cold. The process should last no longer than six weeks. Some

breeds, such as Poodles, have non-shedding coats.

Other influences may cause a dog to lose his hair. Temperature and daylight hours influence the pituitary gland in the brain, and a series of hormonal controls influence coat growth. Dogs that live most of their life indoors are exposed to long periods of artificial light, giving a constant 'photo-period'; combined with evenly regulated temperatures with the central heating, such indoor dogs may shed their coat all the year round. Another hormonal control example is the bitch that will shed her coat six to eight weeks after the birth of puppies; a new coat may take up to four months to regain its full density.

Endocrine disorders that affect the coat may be due to an excess of a body hormone or an insufficient secretion by one of these internal glands. Hormone diseases may make dogs bald; a diagnosis is required for specific treatment. Endocrine disorders

Ringworm on the nose of a West Highland White Terrier.

such as hypothyroidism, Cushing's syndrome, excess oestrogens or insufficient oestrogen in older, spayed bitches are all associated with hair loss and need specific therapies. Thyroid disease causes loss of hair equally on both sides of the body (symmetrical). There is little itching but the coat is thin and easily falls out when rubbed.

Skin parasites cause itching so that the hair is scratched out or rubbed out by the dog rolling or rubbing. Tests should be made to look for a cause.

Acral pruritic dermatitis occurs as an open sore on the 'wrist' or 'ankle'. It is caused by constant licking by the dog's tongue, which produces hair loss and eventual ulceration. It becomes a habit, and, as well as other possible causes, it can be a sign of stress in the dog.

Zinc responsive dermatosis can be seen as dry, hairless skin areas (see p. 137 under Nutraceuticals).

Treatment: When a dog starts to moult, encourage the removal of dead hair by combing and fingertip massage, rubbing the hand up against the lie of the coat. It would be an advantage to arrange cooler sleeping quarters, and to regulate the amount of light experienced each day by the dog. The judicious use of small quantities of fish liver oil has

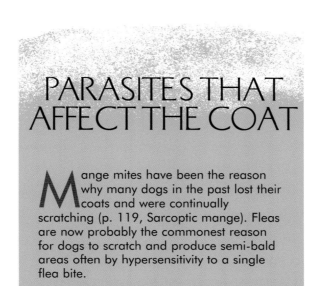

PARASITES THAT AFFECT THE COAT

Mange mites have been the reason why many dogs in the past lost their coats and were continually scratching (p. 119, Sarcoptic mange). Fleas are now probably the commonest reason for dogs to scratch and produce semi-bald areas often by hypersensitivity to a single flea bite.

been used to supplement the vitamin A intake and to bring natural oils back into the dog's skin.

CANINE ATOPY

One of the most frequent diagnoses in skin conditions is atopic dermatitis (AD). It is caused by an immunological hypersensitivity to things like pollen, house dust mites and mould spores – all common in the dog's environment. Atopy probably affects 10-15 per cent of the dog population, and is common in many breeds. An inherited tendency has been demonstrated for Labradors and Golden Retrievers.

The cause of atopy is an exaggerated allergic response. Allergens are usually minute protein particles that penetrate the skin and are detected by body cells that set up a defence

reaction. An overactive response by 'alarm cells' allows the release of histamine and other substances that start off the itchiness in the dog. In a food allergy, a similar effect is found in the intestines, but here the response is more likely to be diarrhoea. Inhaled pollen affects the nose and lungs as another form of hayfever-type allergy.

The general advice is not to breed from affected animals. There are exceptions, and one atopic bitch was able to produce a litter of six healthy, unaffected puppies, all of which were accepted for assistance dog training without any skin problems developing. Atopy may develop in a dog that has been stressed, and this may be experienced in the dog at the age of 18 months to three years when many allergic conditions are most likely to be seen first. Most atopic dogs also develop other problems, such as ear disease, flea allergies and food hypersensitivity. There is always hope for improvement, as many allergic conditions seem to diminish their effects after five years or so as the body adjusts to the factors causing an allergy.

Signs: There are various signs that may first show between six months and three years of age.
• Skin itching known as pruritus: chewing at the feet, ear

A Bull Terrier with skin atopy.

scratching and rubbing the face on the ground are such signs

- Secondary infection with bacteria or yeasts causes red skin patches, which may ooze – pyoderma
- Skin thickening (lichenification), hair loss (alopecia)
- Digestive symptoms, such as vomiting, loose faeces or excessive 'tummy rumbles' (known as borborygmus) develop with food intolerances.

Treatment: A whole range of tests are available to the vet to try to pinpoint the cause of the atopy. Coat brushings, tape tests, intradermal prick tests, blood (ELISA) tests, and diet tests (when it is necessary to eliminate a specified food for six weeks) may be used, but these tests are often not conclusive.

The treatment will be prolonged, and on a 'trial and error' basis, until the most suitable plan of control is found. Antihistamines of various types can be tried; cortisone reduces the itching but has to be used carefully, as it affects many organ systems.

Fatty acid supplementation in the diet helps to build up the skin's own 'lipid barrier', which reduces the allergic reaction. Cyclosporine A, in tablet form, has produced good results in atopy, but it needs careful usage. A series of injections for desensitisation of a protein have also been tried, sometimes with good results.

Flea control is always important, as are other means of dealing with parasites and the pyoderma bacteria.

FURUNCULOSIS & PYODERMA

Furunculosis is the name given to deep-seated skin infection and sometimes the word pyoderma is used for bacteria that penetrate the deeper skin layers. Such chronic local skin infections are found after allergic skin disease and made worse by any loose skin folds. Scratching at itching skin, as found with ringworm or sarcoptic mange, leads to bacteria penetrating the outer skin and producing oozing pockets of infection.

Deep infections require intensive and prolonged treatment. Skin washes (after clipping all matted hair away) and antibiotics are used (which are based on culture and sensitivity tests the vet will perform).

AUTOIMMUNE & IMMUNE-MEDIATED SKIN DISEASES

Autoimmune disorders develop when some parts of the body's tissues are attacked by the dog's own immune system as if they were invading substances. This is seen at its worst when the red cells of the blood are attacked as an antibody – an antigen reaction leading to severe illness known as immune-mediated haemolytic anaemia.

There are several immune-mediated diseases that occur in the skins of dogs and they can develop rapidly. Pemphigus is not common, but antibodies start attacking skin cells, resulting in blisters or ulcers. Dogs look very ill and pyoderma often develops. Biopsies are needed to distinguish various forms of pemphigus. At present, there is no complete cure, but symptoms can be contolled with medication.

ENDOCRINE DISORDERS

Chapter 17

The internal gland control system of the body relies on hormones as chemical messengers. These substances need a trigger factor before they are made in the gland and then released into the body, but will then continue to act slowly for months or years – unlike a nerve impulse, which produces an immediate effect but then wears off unless re-stimulated. Some hormones may be produced in excess in diseased states, or there may be a failure of adequate levels being reached and these states are known as endocrine disease. The most commonly recognised endocrine disease is diabetes (see p. 73). Effects of hormone imbalances can be shown in all parts of the body. In cases of skin disease caused by hormonal upset, such as thyroid deficiency, the hair is lost from one region of the body first, often symmetrical in shape, with a bald patch on one side of the body being the mirror image of the other.

THE THYROID GLAND

This gland is on the underside of the neck, close to the larynx, and only when in a disease state, such as goitre (iodine deficiency), does it enlarge sufficiently for its location to be found. It is a key endocrine gland, producing two distinct hormones that can have profound effects if the output alters through disease. Thyrocalcitonon hormone controls the calcium level of the blood, and is important especially to the bitch feeding puppies when there is a threat of the calcium level becoming too low. Eclampsia (milk fever) causes seizures when the blood calcium levels drop and is an emergency situation – call the vet and temporarily remove the puppies. The over-production or under-production of the hormone thyroxine can cause other severe illnesses.

HYPOTHYROIDISM

This may occur when the gland is underactive; the hormone thyroxine controls the dog's metabolic rate and is also essential for the normal growth of puppies.

Signs: The deficient production of the metabolic hormone may initially be confused with some other disease, as the signs include hair loss from all over the body, with a thickened pigment skin. Dogs are usually slow, lethargic and become overweight. The hair follicles waste away as the hair becomes brittle and falls out; it is not replaced and 90 per cent of the

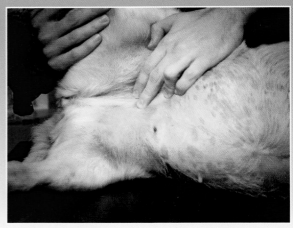

Hair loss in a Yorkshire Terrier with Cushing's disease.

hair follicles are inactive, leaving odd hair tufts still present.

Treatment: Once the diagnosis is confirmed, thyroid hormone can be given each day in tablet form as a permanent replacement therapy.

HYPERTHYROIDISM
Where there is an over-production of the hormone by the thyroid gland, the dog loses weight, is very active and may behave nervously. The dog is always looking for food, is thirsty and may have diarrhoea and vomiting. Again, a poor coat is a sign of this disease. The neck may become swollen, as in goitre or the result of a thyroid cancer.

Treatment: Treatment may be possible and the vet will discuss the options to operate, to use radio-active iodine, or a drug

called methimazole, which is especially effective for cats. It has occasionally been used in dogs with hyperthyroidism.

THE ADRENAL GLANDS
These glands are situated close to the kidneys and produce a number of important hormones.

CANINE CUSHING'S DISEASE
Also known as hyperadrenocorticism (HAC) it is becoming more regularly diagnosed as testing procedures improve. Cortisol over-production may be a response to the stimulating hormone coming from the brain (pituitary gland), adrenal gland tumours (next to the kidneys), or overuse of steroid treatment.

Signs:
• Increased appetite and thirst
• Production of quantities of urine

• A 'pot belly' due to muscle weakness
• The skin becomes thin and wrinkled, hair losses occurring symmetrically on both sides of the body.

Treatment: Veterinary diagnosis to confirm the condition is necessary. Specific treatments for whichever is the cause of the hyperadrenocorticism gives a high degree of success. A tumour of the adrenal may be operated on, or a drug called trilostane (or in the USA mitotane) is available for treatment under close veterinary supervision. The drug blocks the synthesis in the body of sex hormones (such as testosterone and oestradiol) as well as the cortex hormones (glucocorticoids, mineralocorticoids) so must be used with constant monitoring by the vet.

HYPOADRENOCORTICISM

Also known as Addison's disease, this is far less common in dogs. It is the result of inadequate production of cortisone and similar adrenal hormones.

Signs: The signs of hypoadrenocorticism are vague, involving loss of appetite and disinclination to go for walks. There is not an immediate deterioration, but the raising of the blood potassium level can lead to collapse and heart failure.

Treatment: If the dog has collapsed, fluids that are high in salt but low in potassium can be given intravenously, but nursing care to monitor the dog's response is essential. Sometimes cortisone group drugs will be used to correct an imbalance.

OTHER HORMONE DISORDERS

There are other hormone disorders that are quite uncommon. Sex hormone changes may be the result of hypogonadism, where the testes produce insufficient hormone. Hormone imbalances may cause swelling of the nipples and vulva, or a hanging down prepuce in males. Hair losses may occur on the flanks, neck and around the lower abdomen. Again, veterinary diagnostic tests will be necessary. Treatments are available depending on the cause.

PART II

PART III

COMPLEMENTARY THERAPIES

HOLISTIC VETERINARY MEDICINE

Chapter 18

Alternatives to recognised and conventional veterinary treatment have received great attention in recent years. Complementary medicine has become more 'mainstream' and many veterinary surgeons are able to agree that there is a place for some, if not all, of the less conventional types of treatment.

An interest in traditional herbal remedies for canine use has been renewed, as people become more worried about the overuse of antibiotics and the introduction of newly developed 'strong' medication, as well as concerns about possible side effects of conventional medication (often based on human medication experiences).

In the UK, pet insurance companies are usually willing to deal with treatment claims where alternative therapies have been used on a dog. It is always wise to check with the insurer before starting on expensive courses of treatment for any condition. It should also be remembered that an 'excess' sum of money is deducted by the insurer for each individual disorder treated: many therapists may want to treat several conditions at the same time, so care must be taken when filling in a claim to specify one principal disease.

Using alternative and conventional means of diagnosis and therapies, the word 'holistic' implies a wish to cover the comprehensive approach to the care of the dog's health.

Holistic veterinary medicine is approved by most professionals. An account of acupuncture, and herbal (botanical) medicine, chiropractic, homoeopathy, physiotherapy and massage, as well as nutraceuticals, are included here to give an introduction to these topics, but in addition conventional veterinary treatments of pharmaceutical medication, surgical procedures and dentistry may also be considered holistic.

Those who wish to follow specific types of holistic treatment are advised to contact specialist information sources and then research what may be involved.

Conventional medical and veterinary treatments should place greater importance on the relationship between patient and the consultant. More time allowed during the appointment would give time for confidences to develop, with simple explanations of what the person giving the treatment is hoping to achieve.

Complementary medicine may provide the compassion that is occasionally lacking in modern, business-minded small-animal veterinary practice. Dog owners who turn to the internet for information on animal disorders may receive information on unproven and non-scientific ideas on disease and treatments, while a face-to-face interview about the dog should allow time for questions to be asked and answered as well as is possible.

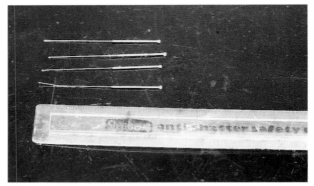

Needles used in acupuncture.

ACUPUNCTURE

The use of acupuncture for veterinary purposes dates back to traditional Chinese medicine. Pao Lo is considered to be the father of Chinese veterinary acupuncture, dating from 480BC. Jesuit missionaries, visiting China and Japan, who brought back news of these acupuncture skills, led to its use in France in the 19th century. Human acupuncture was brought to England in 1821 and by 1828 the first report of its use on animals was printed in *The Veterinarian* magazine. This early journal read by veterinary surgeons reported that 'acupuncture had a great power in relieving many painful and obstinate nervous and muscular affections'. The anonymous writer was quoting on the use of acupuncture at the Paris veterinary college in 1825: of the five animals treated, the only success seems to have been in a dog affected with chorea – the twitching after-effect of an attack of canine distemper. The report

said that after sticking six needles in the dog's thigh, the dog was cured after 21 days.

It can be said that acupuncture has been well tried over the years; but nothing more was written and it was not until the 1970s that Western acupuncture developed. Human charts employing the points used in traditional Chinese medicine (TCM) were then adapted for use with dogs.

BENEFITS FOR ANIMALS

It has been shown that acupuncture works in a number of situations. It is particularly popular for the management of postoperative and chronic pain. Stimulation by placing a needle into the body of the dog at those places known as acupuncture points affects the central neural regulation of the body, causing specific responses. An immune response may result and the puncturing may cause the brain to release endorphins, which are the natural pain killers.

The most popular theory that explains the pain-killing effects of

acupuncture is known as the gate theory. The immune response and inflammatory reaction due to minor trauma to tissue caused by a penetrating acupuncture needle will have a generalised response in the whole body. In humans there is psychological support from the attention given to the patient by the acupuncturist and this may have benefits where there is a human-animal bond present. Briefly this means that when a sensory nerve ending is stimulated by an acupuncture needle, impulses from other pain-carrying nerves are blocked at a 'gate' in the spinal cord so the sensation of pain is not felt at brain level or, if present, it is felt in a modified and acceptable form.

OTHER FACTORS IN TREATMENT

Traditional Chinese medicine (TCM) does not suggest that acupuncture should be the sole treatment used. Diet, exercise, the dog's environment and the use of herbal remedies should all play a part in treatment. Imbalances in the energy level can be produced by external factors such as wind, cold, summer heat, excessive moisture in the air or excess warmth and dryness. Too much or too little physical stress will affect the body's 'humours' as will the irregular intake of food – facts well known to observant humans. Emotional factors seem less appropriate to dogs but it is easy to see the joy in a dog's expression when the possibility of an interesting walk is on offer! The adjustment of energy levels by the stimulation of the designated acupuncture points or a number of associated points can allow a homoeostatic condition (when the body 'resets' itself so that all the major organs are working in balance with each other and healing can take place more quickly).

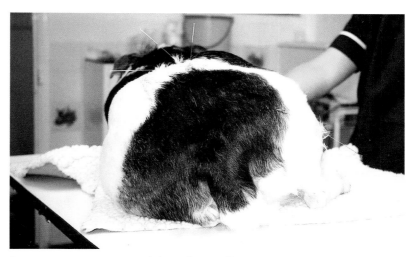

Acupuncture on an overweight Jack Russell Terrier.

WHEN TO USE ACUPUNCTURE

There are about 350 points on the body where acupuncture needles can be inserted, and a lengthy period of study by the acupuncturist is necessary to know how and when to use these. Acupuncture is regularly used on a wide range of conditions where conventional treatment has failed to produce a response. Allergy, dermatoses, lick granuloma of the legs, chronic breathing problems, gastrointestinal disorders, and many conditions where chronic pain affects the dog's behaviour and temperament are all situations where acupuncture may be tried.

The most common use of acupuncture in dogs is for nerve disorders and bone conditions: paresis and paralysis from intervertebral disc disease being one of the most successful if not spectacular uses of veterinary acupuncture. Pain caused by hip

dysplasia, osteochondrosis, spinal disabilities and many other arthritic conditions can all benefit the dog from the use of acupuncture. A recent development in therapy is to use 'photonic energy' in the form of light instead of needles at the acupuncture points. Reiki (p. 132) has been developed in dogs as another alternative to the use of needles puncturing the body.

The dog owner resorting to acupuncture must obtain a veterinary diagnosis before treatment begins. Correct diagnosis is essential. Acupuncture used on its own might delay the treatment of a potentially life-threatening disorder – cancer and severe blood-clotting disorders are unlikely to be cured quickly by acupuncture when specific treatments are available for a confirmed disease. Removing

pain may encourage the dog to become active and delay the healing of the original bone injury or other problem. Pain has a protective function to encourage rest or immobility.

CHIROPRACTIC TREATMENT

The word 'chiropractic' means 'done by hand' and it is considered safe when performed by skilled persons: spinal manipulation was an ancient and trusted art. Today, dogs can benefit from chiropractic treatment for diseases of the muscles and bones. Modern McTimoney techniques (a particular form of chiropractic treatment) are applied to large and small animals. The 1994 Chiropractic Act of Parliament in the UK governs the sector. The letters AMC after the name indicate that the person is skilled in treating animal disorders.

PART III

REIKI

As a traditional art, it is fortunate that there are now veterinary surgeons and veterinary nurses who have trained and specialised in this treatment of dogs. Reiki means 'universal force', originating in Japan as a form of spiritual healing. The human practitioner of Reiki is a channel to draw on the universal life force – reiki – which then helps the body, the mind and the spirit to heal, it is claimed. Reiki is used as a complementary treatment with orthodox medicine but care must be taken to find an accredited practitioner, preferably a Master of Reiki.

The practitioner of Reiki puts their hands on or over the dog, but it involves no manipulation, fulfilling the doctor's Hippocratic oath 'never to do injury or harm'.

When Reiki is used on a nervous animal, the subject will start to relax after a few minutes, often with a puzzled facial expression or glazed eyes. There is no scientific explanation for the process but this is not unusual in alternative medicine. One suggestion is that the healer stimulates the dog's brain to synthesise the neuro-transmitter dopamine. The internal secretion, similar to a massage, has a deeply relaxing effect, eases stress and gives an observed calming. There are even internet sources that claim to be able to do this for your dog, but from a long distance the only possible benefit is through the owner's faith in the procedure, with the dog in some way responding to cues given by the motivated owner.

Intervertebral disc disorders are not uncommon in some breeds of dogs (p. 99). The correct alignment of the vertebrae bones of the spine is vital to maintain the nerve pathways. Pain may result from pressure on nerves or paralysis in severe cases. The chiropractic practitioner will palpate all the bones and joints of the body to look for imbalance but will usually turn attention to the spine. Rapid fingertip pressure is then used, as a quick thrust, to allow a bone to settle back into its normal or regular situation. No forceful stretching or pressure is required in the adjustment of bones and this treatment can, therefore, be considered very safe in dogs.

MAGNETOTHERAPY

This has been used on dogs to relieve pain and increase mobility. Magnets of either ceramics or neomydium have been used and instructions are given to arrange the magnetic field for 'central reverse polarity' so that electrons in the body are actively moved. There is no scientific proof that such magnetic field therapy benefits dogs. Solid tumours in mice were shrunk by the use of magnets in the laboratory using far more powerful fields than obtainable by smaller magnets.

There could be a place for lining up electrons with magnets to treat disease but proof is still required.

A more effective way of applying magnetic therapy is by pulsing low-frequency magnetism using battery-powered packs applied direct to the animal. Such pulsed electromagnetic fields (PEMF) are used in human medicine to stimulate nerve repair and in equine practice there is considerable faith in pulsed magnetic therapy to restore horses to fitness. Some veterinary practitioners use magnetic therapy on animals in combination with acupuncture therapy.

Lodestones, which were natural stones containing iron, were used to navigate ships at sea long before compasses were developed. Historically, honey and ground-up lodestone were used as a paste to apply to diseased parts of the body: when included in this way the energy of the magnet could draw out disease. Cleopatra was reported to wear a lodestone on her forehead to offset the effects of old age: regrettably it did not protect her from death when asps were applied to her body.

The north pole of the magnet decreases bacteria and viruses and is claimed to shrink tumours and decrease inflammation. Conversely, the south pole of the magnet would encourage harmful activities in the body, such as stimulating cell multiplication. Care should therefore be taken in treating dogs with cancer in this way.

Some dogs wear a copper bracelet on their leg, often provided by an owner who has benefited from magnetic field therapy. It is even possible to purchase bandages with copper wire threaded in the cloth, which would have the same effect.

Another form of the treatment, radionics, is performed by a remote practitioner and relies on electromagnetic fields in the

Some people believe that magnetotherapy aids the healing process when a dog has been injured.

earth. The idea grew up that each animal has its own electromagnetic field, which, if distorted, will result in a disease. It was suggested that by sending a few hairs or a spot of blood to the radionics practitioner, he or she could set his or her mind to the disease history so that with extrasensory perception (ESP) one can discover the underlying course of the disease process. At one time it might have been considered laughable that one spot of blood or a saliva mouth swab could be used to confirm parentage or even the presence of hereditary disease through DNA analysis. If treatment can be recommended by a practitioner

to remove adverse factors, then it is the dog owner's own decision whether to follow it.

PHYSIOTHERAPY

In the specific area of rehabilitation, this range of treatments for dogs that complement conventional treatment, is being increasingly used. The use of massage as a form of therapy in animal treatments has been established for over a hundred years, but it is only recently that degree courses in physiotherapy for restoring mobility and reducing pain in animals became available. Physiotherapy uses any physical or mechanical methods, such as massage, heat, exercise or electricity. The Association of Chartered Physiotherapists in Animal Therapy (ACPAT) was founded in 1984. Many veterinary nurses have been trained in the principles of physiotherapy too, and treatments may be available in the practice or locally. The National Association of Veterinary Physiotherapists in the UK requires training on a two-year course before practising is allowed. Any person can perform physical therapy so care should be taken when selecting treatment to obtain an experienced person. There may well be a choice of

Hydrotherapy provides effective non-weight bearing exercise.

treatments: manual therapy or electrotherapy to assist recovery, as well as therapeutic ultrasound, laser treatments, and electrical muscle stimulation. The physiotherapist will look at an injury as a repairable process rather than an event needing a cure. The injured part should be able to regain full function and the removal of pain will restore a dog's activity much quicker than an equivalent human injury where there may be social or other reasons not to be fully active again.

LASERS & ULTRASOUND

Therapeutic lasers are an effective tool used in physiotherapy. They can work on the lymph, circulatory and nervous systems. They are also of value in post-operative care after surgery. The depth of penetration is increased when gentle pressure is applied to the laser diode held against the skin. Ultrasound is a heat-producing process. The sound waves transfer their energy to the molecules they pass through and can help the repair of deep tissues.

HYDROTHERAPY

Hydrotherapy has become very popular. It involves the dog swimming in a properly constructed pool and it is an activity even the oldest pet can enjoy. Many hydrotherapy centres offer swimming as a method of non-weight bearing exercise for the management of arthritic and dysplastic conditions, as well as for muscle conditioning or obesity management. The Canine Hydrotherapy Association governs the use of special dog clinics that help to restore normal use to damaged tissues and stiff joints. Heart function and circulation can be improved by the warm bath; underwater treadmills help a dog to exercise in shallow water. Dog hydrotherapy employs water temperatures of 28C (80F) to help muscle relaxation.

HOME TREATMENTS

There are many other simple physiotherapy measures a dog owner can use where heat is applied in various ways as a traditional treatment. Heat can be applied in one of two forms: By treating the skin surface parts or by heating the deeper tissues of the body. Hot cloths, infra red lamps, and electrical heating pads will only penetrate the skin surface to a depth of one centimetre.

Cryotherapy is the application of cold to anywhere on the body to decrease blood flow. It slows the release of chemicals that cause pain and inflammation. Cold is important in physiotherapy if used immediately after an injury. An ice pack should be applied for the first 15 minutes after an injury (such as a sprain) has been noticed. It is essential not to leave an ice pack on an area of the body too long, as it could stop blood flowing: in an area with little fat or skin muscle, 10 minutes is long enough. Cold and pressure to a joint cause blood vessels to narrow and a reduction in tissue metabolism. These help to limit swelling and toxic tissue damage. Cold decreases sensitivity of the nerves

PART III

in that spot and reduces the ability of nerves to conduct messages to the brain. After an injury, pain and muscle spasm generally follow any musculo-skeletal damage, and pressure on the nerve endings can be reduced by the application of cold. Ice massage too can be used.

HOMOEOPATHY

Homoeopathic medicine is based on the idea that an illness can be cured by using minute doses of a substance that produces symptoms similar to those shown by the canine patient. There are experienced veterinary surgeons who practise homoeopathy and it is not difficult for the dog owner to obtain a referral to attend one of these specialised clinics.

It is also possible for the dog owner to obtain homoeopathic medicines to use on their own dog. Homoeopathy has few side effects so can be called a safe method of home treatment. There may be some worsening of the symptoms before an improvement is seen – so a good length of time should be allowed before deciding if this is the right treatment for the dog. If a dog is on conventional medication, such as non-steroidal anti-inflammatories or even

JOINT MOBILISATION AND STRETCHING

The use of other forms of physiotherapy is best left to the trained person who will assess the dog's problem before deciding on which one of many treatments to use. Following massage to relax and warm the muscles, other methods can be used to mobilise stiff joints and stretch the soft tissue around the joints. Stretching is a very good exercise but pulling at the leg, back or neck can be harmful and should not exceed the pain-free range of movements. The most frequently used technique is passive stretching, where the joint is stretched (known as hyerextension or hyperflexion) and held for 15 to 30 seconds. These stretches may be repeated up to 20 times in a session. Stop treatment if you are causing pain.

cortisone (as for arthritis), this may not allow a homoeopathic remedy to work. A decision may have to be made whether to abandon prescribed medicine before starting on homoeopathy and this can be detrimental to the older dog with conditions such as arthritis where pain may be experienced.

The supply of homoeopathic remedies for animals with accompanying instruction booklets was available over one

hundred years ago. It is equally easy to consult lists of all medical conditions in domestic pets and an equivalent homoeopathic remedy is listed. The use of the internet has made this readily available. Some chronic disorders where cures have been effected include dermatological, autoimmune, gastrointestinal, musculoskeletal and neurological conditions. In acute conditions there should be caution, as denying an animal the benefit of specific drugs for an infection could lead to the loss of a life. However, there are good reports of homoeopathy in the use of less life-threatening infections, such as kennel cough. As well as information from books and health food stores selling remedies, the internet is now a very useful source of information on which remedy to use in which situation.

ALTERNATIVES TO VACCINATIONS

There is a growing feeling that vaccinations may be harmful – in that a foreign substance is being injected in to the dog's body. The Gloucestershire general practitioner Dr Jenner first used vaccination after he saw the devastation to the skin of

PART III

young people who had been afflicted by smallpox. At that time smallpox left many young people with rough, pock-marked faces, which in the case of village girls affected their chances of a satisfactory marriage. Dr Jenner's use of scabs from the teats of cows affected by 'cowpox' to inoculate people turned out to be one of the greatest scientific advances of the 18th Century.

Lady Mary Montagu Wortley had introduced a means of treating smallpox, before Edward Jenner. She recommended (but did not actually employ) 'innoculation': an exceedingly dangerous practice of transferring live infected scabs from a smallpox victim to people hoping to gain protection from the disfiguring disease. Altering the nature of a bacteria or a virus and giving it in a weakened form represents the basis of all protective vaccines.

In human medicine homoeopathy practitioners may advise their clients against vaccination and the choice is a personal one. For animals the choice is the owners' and it is known that nosodes (homoeopathic alternatives to vaccines) have failed to protect dogs from death due to parvoviral enteritis. Nosodes are prepared from highly diluted preparations of diseased material, and, as such, are not prepared

Increasingly dog owners are turning towards complementary therapies as a positive approach to health care.

according to homoeopathic principles (being better described as 'isopathy', as the active ingredient is derived from animal origins). Nosodes would appear to be effective as long as enough other people are using conventional vaccines to protect the majority of the dog population. However if the use of such nosode agents of 'protection' became widespread, as soon as the non-vaccinated population of dogs is large enough to allow virulent agents to spread, disease outbreaks such as the ravages of distemper may reoccur.

The use of homoeopathic alternatives to vaccines is an attempt to replicate the same

stimulation of the immune system to an unwanted disease by using a nosode. A dog's immune system provides protection from disease, but it may fail. Boosting the immune system to make the body able to resist disease is a valuable activity and the less reliance of antibiotics to combat any disease that has entered the body, the better.

Nosodes prepared from high dilutions of infectious agents, or from discharges, vomit or faecal matter are not prepared on strict homoeopathic principles. The British Faculty of Homoeopathy acknowledges the effectiveness of the conventional vaccines and in humans recommends their use. Some veterinary homoeopathists are strongly against dogs receiving annual booster vaccines but it is difficult to judge when not to protect a dog if good, safe vaccines are available.

HERBAL MEDICINE

A growing interest in traditional ways of curing disease is partially a result of some of the tragedies reported when powerful new drugs have caused unexpected side effects or death. Botanical medicine, as it is known, was the only treatment available as

NUTRACEUTICAL MEDICINE

Therapeutic nutrition plays an important part in healing and recovery from disease. Nutraceutical medicine is defined as the use of micronutrients, macronutrients and other nutritional supplements as agents for the treatment of illnesses. It should also be noted that all bitter herbs improve the assimilation of nutrients and can be incorporated into the feeding regime (see p. 138).

VITAMINS

Antioxidants are beneficial and include vitamins E and C, taurine, lycopene, Beta carotene and lutein, which are found in many vegetable diets. Fatty acids, such as those found in fish oils, are of value, especially in skin conditions, joint mobility and in suppressing inflammation.

The use of vitamin E as an anti-oxidant has been of benefit in heart conditions, Selenium is closely associated with vitamin E. Dogs, unlike humans, can make their own supply of vitamin C in their intestines. There are times when extra vitamin C in the diet can be beneficial, such as for stimulating the immune system.

The water-soluble vitamin L-carnitine is used in dogs with dilated cardiomyopathy (see p. 81) but first received much attention in cats when a dietary deficiency produced a disease known as hepatic lipidosis. It can be important too for the older dog showing signs of stiffness, muscle weakness and cramps. Deficiency can cause muscle disorders known as lipid storage myopathies and a powder supplement can be given thrice daily, although some foods now contain L-carnitine supplements.

JOINT CARE

Glucosamines have recently come into prominence as being important in the prevention and treatment of arthritis.

Glycosaminoglycans are large molecules found inside joints that help lubricate the joint fluid with corresponding reduction in pain and increased mobility. These compounds can be used in older dogs; some of the manufactured foods now contain such supplements.

DIGESTIVE HEALTH

Probiotics are microbial preparations given by mouth that pass through to the intestines. As they are beneficial bacteria, they can supply nutrients (such as vitamin B12) to the dog, aid in digestion and produce better food absorption. Their use is advised in recovery from enteric conditions, such as parvovirus, and may be given as a powder supplement to help recovery in many disorders.

HEALTHY SKIN & COAT

Zinc is an essential trace element for dogs. It is found as metalloenzymes that control many of the body's activities. Some breeds, such as Alaskan Malamutes, Siberian Huskies and Bull Terriers, are said to be affected by inherited metabolic disorders. Other breeds of dog that are more likely to develop a zinc deficiency including Beagles, Dobermanns, German Shepherds, German Shorthaired Pointers, Great Danes, Labrador Retrievers, Rhodesian Ridgebacks and Standard Poodles.

There are many reasons why a dog may need a zinc supplement, but common signs include a dull, rough coat, other skin disorders and sometimes bowel disease. Zinc deficiency may be seen in older dogs and is often associated with vomiting, chronic infections and weight loss. Vegetable diets with a high phytate content could interfere with zinc absorption by the dog. A minimum intake of 9.7 mg/100kcal ME food is advised.

PART III

Aloe vera is widely reported to help with wound healing and burns.

Lavender oil is known for its calming effect.

part of the healer's art until the late 18th century. Country people had to use the plants and herbs that were available to them. William Withering in 1785, (just six years before the opening of the first English-speaking veterinary college) reputedly identified foxglove in a remedy being used by a village woman who treated dropsy successfully by a concoction of many herbs picked in the hedgerow. The cardiotonic digitalis glycosides are still in use to treat congestive heart failure and to slow the heart rate when atrial fibrillation is present.

Few doctors would disagree that herbs have pharmaceutical actions that can be useful and safe. Herbal preparations were in use on a regular basis in orthodox medicine until the 1950s and now pharmaceutical research is directed to find an effective drug from a natural source. The application of herbal medicines increases steadily. Although Chinese medicine evolved to incorporate such techniques as acupuncture, pulse diagnosis etc., interest in herbs and medicinal plants did not cease.

NATURAL HEALING

It is now possible to search the internet for medicinal plants of the world and to find sources of information on the folk use of plants. In veterinary medicine there are some tried-and-trusted remedies:

- Aloe vera for wound healing
- Evening Primrose oil for skin problems
- Arnica for bruises and muscle pain
- Valerian as a sedative
- Tea tree oil is incorporated in some pet shampoos to repel fleas
- Lavender oil is used in aromatherapy for its calming effect, while its use in dog behaviour problems illustrates newer applications of herbal medicine in everyday events.

Herbs can be used for convalescence, a word that has almost been forgotten in human and animal illness. It is the important time after an operation or an infection when the body restores itself to normal health. Although animals are like children who become ill – they appear to make a rapid recovery and want to play again – there is still the need for longer periods of rest and a time for the body to repair.

An example of this was seen in the routine neutering of bitches that were in the process of becoming guide dogs for the blind. Within a few days of spaying, a major abdominal operation, they were at the front of the dog cage wanting to go

SOME RECOMMENDATIONS FOR THE SAFE USE OF HERBAL MEDICINES IN DOGS

For dogs with a heart murmur that you don't want to use drugs for (see innocent heart murmur, p. 82) , the tincture of crataegus can be helpful and it can also be used in the later stages with cardiovascular drugs, as it acts as a 'normaliser' and has a hypotensive effect. Crataegus is the hawthorn. The preparation comes from the tree berries that are turned into a liquid decoction or a tincture.

Animals that are given corticosteroids for a variety of complaints may be giving concern to their owners who are aware of side effects with the use of such drugs. The use of liquorice *Glyerrhiza glabra* as a tincture may allow a reduction in the dose of steroid needed to control a condition. The same herbal remedy helps a dog that has to come off steroids since there is a withdrawal phase whilst the adrenal gland cortex returns to normal secretion. It is advised that liquorice is used for six weeks then treatment stopped for two weeks, then, if required, a further six week treatment with the herbal product is possible. Most of the liquorice sold by confectioners consists of molasses and flour, but for herbal use one needs the preparations made from the root or rhizome of the plant. Liquorice is also a widely used remedy for coughs and lung complaints. It has been described as 'incredibly soothing ' for dogs with a harsh dry cough such as kennel cough (see p. 85).

out again. Dog trainers working to a production schedule would want to get them back into work as soon as possible, even while they still had abdominal wound stitches holding their skin and muscles together. The veterinarian was able to insist on a ten-day recovery period before full work was resumed. Calendula ointment could be used to stimulate wound repair and 'epithelialisation' after an operation where the skin is broken. It is easy to forget that tissues need to repair and muscles grow strong again after surgery, even though the dog may, from outward appearances, appear normal.

Calendula, often known as garden marigold or pot marigold, is one of the safest herbs to use and has a wide range of actions. The orange or yellow petals are best picked as they 'reflex' or start to droop. A hot water infusion of the ray flowers or the whole head can be used for gastrointestinal problems, colitis and diarrhoea.

Calendula tincture is made from the whole plant not just the petals, which are used by homeopaths. Incorporating the tincture into a simple ointment base can make a very good salve for wounds. It has a pleasant yellow to orange colour. Alternatively, a gauze pad can be soaked in the 25-per-cent strength calendula tincture and applied directly to a wound to promote epithelial repair. If an antifungal action is needed as well, the 96-per-cent tincture can be applied as long as the skin remains unbroken.

PART III

It is important to consult a vet before embarking on a course of complementary therapy.

PART III

ADMINISTERING HERBAL TREATMENT

Teas are probably the best known form of herbal treatment, since boiling water will draw out the active constituents of many herbs. Such a tea can be poured over the dog's regular food and some dogs enjoy the earthy flavours produced. Alcoholic tinctures are also popular since their first use in monasteries, when monks used this method of extracting the essential ingredients from leaves, young stems or flower petals. It is important to know the dilution rates of tinctures. Made up with alcohol the most potent are 1:2 dilution rates while a cheaper product found on sale may be 1:5 or more. Tinctures can be administered with the dog food. If the dose is first put in a cup of

hot water it drives much of the alcohol away and the rest of the fluid can then be poured over the dog's normal food. It is rare that a dog objects to these natural odours on the food and it is an easy way of administrating medication.

Aromatic waters are also available from herbal chemists and these are more likely to be readily consumed than essential oil tinctures by some dogs. If there should be an acceptability problem, mix the daily dose of tincture into one teaspoonful of slippery elm.

Comfrey that grows wild was also known as knitbone. Before fracture healing was understood, wrapping a large plant leaf around a damaged limb was almost the only treatment available – reduction and

stabilisation of fractures was unheard of in those times. Comfrey, *Symphytum officinale*, does now have an internal use when a 25-per-cent tincture can be given for coughs, but again it should be used for no more than six weeks at a time. A prescription from a veterinary herbalist might contain several of these plant derivatives in a single prescription.

Herbs can be used to cool and soothe the skin, applied as infusions or creams. Witch hazel is safe and popular as a lotion, but chickweed, chamomile, calendula, and aloe have all been used successfully.

Where a dog is receiving treatment for conditions such as liver or kidney failure, great care should be taken in using alternative herbal therapy since some herbal compounds affect the enzymes in the liver with potentially life-threatening results. Consultation with the veterinary surgeon should be a requisite before using certain herbal products on sick animals.

AROMATHERAPY

Olfaction (the sense of smell)is the oldest method of communication between animals. It evolved from primitive animals seeking food but then developed as a way of signalling by the use of body chemical odorants. Pheromones are used to give messages to other animals, but many plant-based odours can produce very similar responses.

Aromatherapy uses plant oils in a medical way; they can be applied to the skin or more often by absorption through the nose. Aromatic compounds may be wafted near a dog's nose or nebulised as a fine spray in the air that will be breathed.

CRYSTAL THERAPY

Crystal therapy has a few supporters as an alternative method of healing animals and is mentioned here as another aspect of complementary therapy. Warm coloured stones were said to stimulate energy flow whilst the cool colours calmed over-activity. It was believed the animal body had seven chakras that could be altered by the influence of healing stones. Crystals could be placed in the pet's bed or held in the owner's hand near to appropriate chakras if this type of treatment is used.

Essential oils can be obtained from fruits (especially the outer peel), flowers, leaves, tree bark or resin that exudes from the tree trunk. The aromatherapist will choose the products that from experience are most suited to the dog's state.

Conditioning a dog to an odour can be a reminder of a dog's previous calm and secure state. Animals mark the limits of their territory by smells: faeces and urine are the most common substances, but the foot pads and tail glands secrete distinctive odours also. The mammary glands of the bitch exude a pheromone that calms puppies and is associated with milk feed repletion. This substance has been produced artificially and is marketed as Dog Appeasing Pheromone (DAP) to use where dogs are under stress. Similar plant products can be used: lavender oil is one of several essential oils used to calm dogs. A dog collar that gives a puff of lemon smell every time the dog barks is the use of a smell as an aversive training aid. Peppermint contains menthol, which can have a similar deterrent effect, but when used as a vaporised volatile oil it is beneficial in dogs with gastro-enteritis. Dogs may react positively to the use of valerian oil for its sedative effect, but if used by humans, it can be a notoriously unpleasant effect.

INDEX